Jez Butterworth

JERUSALEM

NICK HERN BOOKS

London

www.nickhernbooks.co.uk

Jerusalem was first performed at the Royal Court Theatre Downstairs, London, on 15 July 2009 (previews from 10 July), with the following cast (in order of appearance):

PHAEDRA	Aimeé-Ffion Edwards
MS FAWCETT	Sarah Moyle
MR PARSONS	Harvey Robinson
JOHNNY 'ROOSTER' BYRON	Mark Rylance
GINGER	Mackenzie Crook
PROFESSOR	Alan David
LEE	Tom Brooke
DAVEY	Danny Kirrane
PEA	Jessica Barden
TANYA	Charlotte Mills
WESLEY	Gerard Horan
DAWN	Lucy Montgomery
MARKY	Lewis Coppen/ Lennie Harvey
TROY WHITWORTH	Barry Sloane

Director	Ian Rickson
Designer	Ultz
Lighting Designer	Mimi Jordan Sherin
Sound Designer	Ian Dickinson for Autograph
Composer	Stephen Warbeck

The production transferred to the Apollo Theatre, London, on 10 February 2010 (previews from 28 January), with the same cast and creative team, except for the following roles:

DAWN	Amy Beth Hayes
MARKY	Charlie Dunbar-Aldred/ Lennie Harvey/Jake Noble

It was produced by Sonia Friedman Productions, Royal Court Theatre Productions, Old Vic Productions, in association with Robert G. Bartner/Norman Tulchin, Lee Menzies and Rupert Gavin.

The play received its North American premiere at the Music Box Theatre, New York, on 21 April 2011 (previews from 2 April), with the original London cast and creative team, except for the following roles:

LEE	John Gallagher Jr.
PEA	Molly Ranson
WESLEY	Max Baker
DAWN	Geraldine Hughes
MARKY	Mark Page/Aiden Eyrick

It was produced by Sonia Friedman Productions, Stuart Thompson, Scott Rudin, Roger Berlind, Royal Court Theatre Productions, Beverly Bartner/Alice Tulchin, Dede Harris/Rupert Gavin, Broadway Across America, Jon B. Platt, 1001 Nights/Stephanie P. McClelland, Carole L. Haber/Richard Willis, Jacki Barlia Florin/Adam Blanshay.

The production returned to the Apollo Theatre, London, on 17 October 2011 (previews from 8 October), with the original London cast and creative team, except for the following roles:

LEE	Johnny Flynn
PEA	Sophie McShera
WESLEY	Max Baker
DAWN	Geraldine Hughes
MARKY	Lennie Harvey/
	Dylan Standen/
	Archie Waite

It was produced by Royal Court Theatre Productions and Sonia Friedman Productions, in association with Old Vic Productions, Robert G. Bartner/Norman Tulchin and Rupert Gavin.

4

Characters
in order of appearance

PHAEDRA
MS FAWCETT
MR PARSONS
JOHNNY 'ROOSTER' BYRON
GINGER
PROFESSOR
LEE
DAVEY
PEA
TANYA
WESLEY
DAWN
MARKY
TROY WHITWORTH

For Gilly

PROLOGUE

*A curtain with the faded Cross of St George. A proscenium
adorned with cherubs and woodland scenes. Dragons. Maidens.
Devils. Half-and-half creatures. Across the beam:*

– THE ENGLISH STAGE COMPANY –

*A drum starts to beat. Accordions strike up. Pipes. The lights
come down. A fifteen-year-old girl, PHAEDRA, dressed as a
fairy, appears on the apron. She curtsies to the boxes and sings,
unaccompanied.*

PHAEDRA.
> And did those feet in ancient time,
> Walk upon England's mountains green,
> And was the holy lamb of God,
> On England's pleasant pastures seen.

She beams, pulls a string and the wings flap.

> And did the Countenance Divine,
> Shine forth upon those clouded hills,
> And was Jerusalem builded here,
> Among those dark satanic –

Thumping music. She flees. The curtain rises upon...

ACT ONE

England at midnight. A clearing in a moonlit wood. At the back of the clearing stands an old forty-foot mobile home. The deafening bass pumps from within, and from speakers on the roof. People dancing wildly, with abandon. Through the windows we can glimpse more people dancing. They're shouting to be heard, but we can't hear what.

Blackout. Music continues, until...

Birdsong.

Now we can see that the mobile home stands in a fairly permanent state. The old Wessex flag (a golden Wyvern dragon against a red background) flies from one end. An old rusted metal railway sign screwed to the mobile home reads 'Waterloo'.

A porch stands out front – an old mouldy couch stands on the porch deck. Lots of junk. An old hand-cranked air-raid siren. Stuck to the porch post is an old submarine klaxon. An old record player, with a stand-alone speaker. An old American-style fridge. Stacks of old LPs.

Underneath, a chicken coop. Chopped wood under a lean-to. Rubbish. Empty bottles. A car seat, a swing. An old windchime. A garden table, and four red Coca-Cola plastic chairs. A rusty Swingball set.

In the middle of the copse, the remains of a smashed television.

A man, PARSONS, in a suit with a reflective jacket and case enters the copse. He takes a photograph of the smashed television. Another of the mess on the table. He gingerly picks his way to the front door.

He is followed by a woman, FAWCETT, dressed the same. With a clipboard. She surveys the clearing.

FAWCETT. Time.

PARSONS. Eight fifty-nine and fifty-five. Six. Seven. Nine o'clock.

She nods. He knocks on the door.

Mr Byron? Mr John Byron? Johnny Byron? (*Knocks.*) John Rooster Byron.

FAWCETT (*rebuking*). Parsons.

PARSONS (*apologetic*). Ma'am.

FAWCETT. Stand back.

He does.

Mr Byron? (*She knocks.*) Mr Byron? Would you care to step outside for a moment? (*Pause. Knocks.*) Mr Byron? (*Pause.*) We know you're in there, Byron. Would you give us a moment of your time? Would you like to step outside and face the music for me?

Silence. A distant church bell rings nine. She touches up her lipstick. PARSONS removes a digital video camera from his bag.

Ready?

PARSONS. Rolling.

FAWCETT. Linda Fawcett, Kennet and Avon Senior Community Liaison Officer. 9 a.m., 23rd April. Serving Notice F-17003 in contravention of the Public Health Act of 1878, and the Pollution Control and Local Government Order 1974.

Loud barking can be heard from inside.

PARSONS. I never knew he had –

FAWCETT. He doesn't.

PARSONS. But –

FAWCETT. That is not a dog, Parsons.

The barking gets louder. More ferocious.

Very funny, Mr Byron. Extremely amusing.

Louder still. Snarling.

PARSONS. Are you sure?

FAWCETT. Shut up, Parsons.

PARSONS. Rolling –

Plaintive howling throughout. A hatch opens on the top of the mobile home. A head appears, wearing a Second World War helmet and goggles, with loudhailer, like out of the top of a tank. Barking. The camera pans up to it. It disappears sharply.

FAWCETT. Under Section 62 of the Criminal Justice and Public Order Act, supported by Order 24, the County Court ruling which was heard in Salisbury County Court on 12th March –

The loudhailer appears out of a window at the side of the vehicle to the blind side of the camera and barks over:

– and also employs the use of Order 113 of the Rules of the County Court. With the aforementioned notice, Kennet and Avon include a brochure outlining Unauthorised Encampment Policy, the Strategy and Partnership Section, issue date December 2002, reference 4.06.0001006.

She removes a piece of paper and a staple gun. She goes over to the front door and solemnly staples the page to the door. Four, five times.

(*Calling out through the crack in the door.*) Goodbye, Mr Byron. And see you tomorrow at 9 a.m. sharp, sir. (*She turns.*) Parsons.

She leads the way.

PARSONS (*to himself*). I'll say this. It's a lovely spot.

They leave. A man of about fifty, JOHNNY, *sticks his head out the top of the trailer. He has the loudhailer.*

JOHNNY. Testing. Testing, one two. This is Rooster Byron's dog, Shep, informing Kennet and Avon Council to go fuck itself. Woof woof!

The hatch shuts. Impossibly fast, the front door opens and the same man appears. Wiry. Weathered; drinker's mug. Bare chest. Helmet. Goggles. Loudhailer. Despite a slight limp, he moves with the balance of a dancer, or animal.

Hear ye, hear ye. With the power invested in me by Rooster Johnny Byron – who can't be here on account of the fact he's in Barbados this week with Kate Moss – I, his faithful hound Shep, hereby instruct Kennet and Avon to tell Bren Glewstone, and Ros Taylor, and her twat son, and all those sorry cunts on the New Estate, Rooster Byron ain't going nowhere. Happy St George's Day. Now kiss my beggar arse, you Puritans!

In one practised move he lets off an unexpected airhorn blare into the loudhailer, a long blast. And with that he hangs the loudhailer on a hook (like he does this every day), lifts his goggles, throws the needle on the record player, flicks the 'V's in their general departing direction. He turns and heads across the clearing, just as a crackly 45 of 'Somebody Done Changed the Lock On My Door' by Champion Jack Dupree crackles out of the two speakers strapped to the top of the mobile home.

He yawns his way over to a trough, takes off his helmet, scoops up water and pours it over his face. Shakes himself awake. No good. He kneels and sticks his head in the trough.

Heads back across. Stops. Picks something up. Holds it up to the light. A dropped spliff. He pops it behind his ear. Opens the chicken coop, fishes around for an egg.

On the table on the deck, he picks up a pint glass from several. It's got about ten cigarette butts floating in two inches of golden gunk. He tosses it. Opens the fridge. Takes

*out a pint of milk. Sniffs it. Pours half the milk in. Takes a
half-bottle of vodka out of his arse pocket, pours half of it
into the glass. From the goggle-strap on his helmet he takes a
wrap of speed, rips it in two, sprinkles it in. Cracks the egg
into the glass, swirls it and drinks it down in one. He lets out
a long, feral bellow, from the heart of the earth.*

*He lights the spliff, and stalks across the clearing, doing
steps, and ends up over to the side of the clearing as the song
ends, pissing up against a tree, his back to us.*

I dreamt all night of waterfalls. (*Beat.*) Riches. Fame. A
glimpse of God's tail… Comes a time you'd swap it all for a
solid golden piss on English soil.

*Distant drumming starts. Accordions. A hundred distant
voices sing:*

VOICES.
    With the merry ring, adieu the merry spring,
    For summer is a-come unto day,
    How happy is the little bird that merrily doth sing,
    In the merry morning of May.

    Unite and unite,
    For summer is a-come unto day,
    And wither we are going we all unite,
    In the merry morning of May!

Enter GINGER, *from behind the trailer, singing:*

GINGER.
    Unite and unite,
    For summer is a-come unto day,
    And wither we are going we all unite,
    In the merry morning of May!

Morning, Rooster!

JOHNNY. Morning, Ginger.

    GINGER *starts robotics, moonwalking and doing 'the
    crouch' all at the same time.*

GINGER (*rapping*).

> It's the fair, it's the Flintock Fair.
> It's the motherfucking Flintock Fair.
> It's the fair, it's the Flintock Fair.
> It's shit. But you love it.

He puts his hand to his ear and air-scratches on an air-turntable, he spins himself round 360-degrees. Instantly stops. Looks around.

Hang on, stop. Stop the bus. What happened? What happened here?

JOHNNY. Where? Nothing.

GINGER. Bollocks. What happened?

JOHNNY. What?

GINGER. Don't give me that.

Beat.

JOHNNY. It was a gathering.

GINGER. Don't look like a gathering.

JOHNNY. Was impromptu. Few people showed up. Snowballed.

GINGER. Why didn't you call?

JOHNNY. Look, don't start. I've got a throbber on.

GINGER. Or text me. Never leave a man on the ground…

JOHNNY. I thought you was busy.

GINGER. Who said… (*Stops.*) Fucking… (*Stops.*) *Sex and the City*, mate. Fuckin' Jools Holland then three hours of Pacman on my phone. Not what you'd call a classic. I thought we was mates.

JOHNNY. We are mates.

GINGER. Then pick up the phone. Or text me.

JOHNNY. Ginger –

GINGER. Well, that's that. I've missed a party. That's one I'll never get back. Cheers. I'm just saying. Cheers. Thanks.

JOHNNY. Look. You want the truth? I was minding my own business. Settling in, spliff, *Antiques Roadshow,* when there's a knock on the door. I get up and I answers, and standing outside are all five birds off of Girls Aloud. They've got a case of Super T, two hundred Rothmans. Five Mars Bars. I try to slam the door but they bum-rush me clean across the kitchenette and onto the bed. Nicky guards the door while Kimberley, Nadine, what's-her-name and the other one go to work. Three hours. Unspeakable acts. Finally I manage to slide out from under Cherry Cole –

GINGER. Cheryl. Cheryl Cole –

JOHNNY. Exactly. I slides out from bottom of the scrum, into to the bog, grab my mobile, text, 'Ginger, for fuck's sake, it's an emergency. It's all kicked off round mine with the Girls Aloud. Come and help me get it shifted.' By this point the girls has worked, they're next door riding on each other. It's a complete waste of time. They could have done that at home. Now they're fucking furious. They're taking turns to shoulder-charge the door. My thumb is hoverin' over 'SEND' when the door flies in, and the rest is history. (*He reaches into his pocket.*) That's what happened. That's all you missed. But don't worry. We saved you one.

He tosses GINGER *a Mars Bar.* GINGER *looks at it, then instinctively drops it as if it's unclean.* JOHNNY *cackles.*

GINGER. So you're barred from The Cooper's, then.

JOHNNY. What?

GINGER (*innocently*). I just bumped into Wesley. Says he's barred you.

JOHNNY. Why?

GINGER. On account of the fracas.

JOHNNY. What fracas?

GINGER. The fracas in the saloon bar last night.

JOHNNY. Bollocks. I had a quiet one. Couple pints. Spun the lemons. Come home.

GINGER. That's not what I heard.

JOHNNY. Right. Hang about. First up, that was not a fracas. Two, even if it was a fracas, it weren't my fault. It was Danny Anstey's fault. I'm in the saloon bar, playing pool. Winner stays on. Danny comes over, slaps down a tenner. I seven-ball him. Double or quits. He racks. I break. Seven-ball him. Next minute he's shovin' me in the chest. Says I moved the black while he was in the bog. Starts creating. Says I been burgling flats up the Wilcot Road. I nicked his mum's PlayStation 3. For a start, I don't know where she lives. Second –

GINGER. That's not the fracas I'm talking about.

Beat.

JOHNNY. What do you mean?

GINGER. Way I heard it, Danny leaves. You sit at the bar. Vodka Red Bull. Vodka Red Bull. Vodka Red Bull. Vodka Red Bull. Stagger to the gents'. Five minutes later, come barrelling out in your birthday suit waving your crown jewels around.

JOHNNY. Bollocks.

GINGER. Exactly. Then you pick up Bob Dance's pug and simulate a lewd act. Then you start humping up against Martha Figgis's barstool saying, 'Come on, you old slapper, how about a floor show?' Then the fracas occurred. (*Beat.*) You rang the bell, everyone's silent, clear your throat, say you never touched Danny's mum's PlayStation, but you did shag her when Danny's dad was away in the Falklands. Making him odds-on *not* Danny's dad, in which case he should show some bloody respect.

Pause.

JOHNNY. Last night, you say. (*Beat.*) It's coming back. No, it is. It is. And I can categorically say that that is bollocks. For a start, I was drinking brandy and Cokes. And I was not starkers. If you examine the CCTV, it clearly shows I had my socks on.

GINGER (*makes the umpire signal*). I think we'll refer that one upstairs.

Mate. It's taken years but you've finally done it. You're barred from every pub in Flintock. Phoenix Arms, you broke the bog. They let you back, you locked Jim's lad in the freezer cabinet.

JOHNNY. And he deserved it. Lippy bastard…

GINGER. Moonrakers, you broke the security camera then a week after they let you back, you pick a fight with a squaddie.

JOHNNY. I never started that. Bloody Rambo…

GINGER. First night back you set fire to the Christmas tree. Royal Oak, you were doing whizz off the bar during the meat raffle. Then on Kiddies' Fun Day you slaughtered a live pig in the car park.

JOHNNY. It was a rural display.

GINGER. With a flare gun.

JOHNNY. That was a bloody big weekend.

GINGER. Congratulations. You got the grand slam. To think they said it would never happen.

Beat.

JOHNNY. Storm in a teacup, mate. You watch. I'll buy Danny a pint, sambuca, pop over The Cooper's, pinch Sue's bum. Butter her up, give her a twinkle, ten quid says I'll be back in the snug by lasties. And when you see me, mine's a brandy and Coke.

PROFESSOR (*off*). Mary! Mary? Are you there? Mary? Mary?

GINGER. Here we go.

JOHNNY. Be nice.

GINGER. Here we fucking go.

JOHNNY. Oi. Play nicely. Ginger –

GINGER. I'm not saying anything.

Enter the PROFESSOR, *smartly dressed, with wellies, through the wood.*

PROFESSOR. Good morning, Mr Byron.

JOHNNY. Morning, Professor. You're up early. You off to the fair then?

PROFESSOR. Indeed. Indeed, Mr Byron. Indeed I'm off to the fair.

He clears his throat.

> To see a strange outlandish fowl,
> A quaint baboon, an ape, an owl,
> A dancing bear, a giant's bone,
> A warlock shift a standing stone,
> A rhymer's jests, a juggler's cheats,
> A tumbler showing cunning feats,
> A morris dance, a puppet play,
> Mad Tom to sing a roundelay,
> All this upon St George's Day!

I was up at first light. I said to the shaving mirror, I said, 'It's ten press-ups, then up Rooster's Wood by breakfast. A lungful of wild garlic, then scurry up Orr Hill to watch the floats gather.' Here we are, and now I've lost the dog. I've looked all over. You haven't seen my Mary pass this way?

JOHNNY. Not this morning, Professor. No…

PROFESSOR. She spies a weasel and that's that. I tracked her through the bracken and bluebells. I'll holler myself hoarse for all the good it'll do. Will she come back? Will she?

JOHNNY. I'm sure she'll bundle up.

PROFESSOR. Of course. Of course. Well, it's very good to see you, Mr Byron. Who's this young lady?

JOHNNY. This is Ginger, Professor. You remember Ginger. From last time.

GINGER. Morning.

PROFESSOR. I remember you. You're in the Maths Faculty?

GINGER. No, mate. I'm a DJ.

JOHNNY. Since when?

GINGER. I'm a DJ.

JOHNNY. He's an unemployed plasterer.

PROFESSOR. I see. Are you pure or applied?

GINGER (*to the* PROFESSOR). Just a tick, mate. (*To* JOHNNY.) Since, right, I'm pencilled in second if 2 Trevs pulls out today, from the car park of The Cooper's at sunset. I got my records in the car. (*To the* PROFESSOR.) Sorry. You were saying.

PROFESSOR. A DJ, eh?

GINGER. That's right, mate.

PROFESSOR. How does that work?

GINGER. Basically, I spin sick beats. Bring the ruckus. Drop the bomb on the people at the back 'cause the people at the back don't take no slack.

PROFESSOR. Fascinating. It's Maureen, isn't it?

GINGER. That's right, mate. Maureen.

PROFESSOR. Maureen Pringle.

GINGER. *Doctor* Maureen Pringle. How do you do?

PROFESSOR. How are you finding the funding cuts over there?

GINGER. I think it's disgraceful. I don't see how we're going to meet our quotas. It's like a sausage factory.

PROFESSOR. Word in the college is 1987 is going to be worse.

JOHNNY. I suggest you bring the ruckus.

GINGER. Just you try and stop me…

PROFESSOR. That's the spirit, Maureen.

JOHNNY. I'll tell you what, Maureen.

GINGER. It's *Doctor* Maureen.

JOHNNY. I'll you what, Doctor. You pop in there, make us two bacon rolls, I'll roll a spliff, we'll spruce up. Get down in time for the floats.

GINGER. Only if you tell him I'm a DJ.

JOHNNY. You're not a DJ.

GINGER. Just say it. Say, 'Ginger is a DJ.'

JOHNNY. I'll never say it.

GINGER. Say it.

JOHNNY. Never.

GINGER. Ginger is a DJ.

JOHNNY. Fuck off.

GINGER. Say it.

JOHNNY. No.

GINGER. Say it.

JOHNNY. No.

GINGER. Say it. Say it.

PROFESSOR. For God's sake, man. Say it. 'Ginger is a DJ.' Ginger is a DJ.

Beat.

GINGER (*points to* JOHNNY). You are a cunt. (*Points to the* PROFESSOR.) You, I like.

PROFESSOR. Perhaps, Doctor Pringle, a drink some time?

GINGER. That would be delightful. I should point out for the record I don't actually have GCSE Maths. But I *do* have a great big hairy cock and balls. If that helps. (*He pats the* PROFESSOR*'s cheek. To* JOHNNY.) Not too much baccy.

JOHNNY. Lots of HP.

GINGER *goes inside and shuts the door.*

PROFESSOR. By God. She's *modern*.

JOHNNY (*unscrews the lid on a flask*). Will you take this Sergeant Major's this morning, Professor?

PROFESSOR. Given the occasion, Mr Byron, anything but Sergeant Major's would be unpatriotic.

JOHNNY. What are we drinking to?

JOHNNY *hands them both a cup of tea. He pours the Scotch in. The* PROFESSOR *raises his tea.*

PROFESSOR.
     To Titania. To Woden's Wild Hunt.
     To the blossom and the May-come,
     St George, and all the lost gods of England!

They drain their cups. Slap them down.

By the way, I saw some people in the wood. Officials. A man and a woman. They were here last week.

JOHNNY. They're from the Palace. The Queen wants to commission a portrait of me to hang in the National Gallery. In recognition for my years of charitable service to the community.

PROFESSOR. Are you quite sure? They looked serious. You're not in trouble, I hope, Mr Byron?

JOHNNY. You don't need to worry yourself, Professor. Not on a beautiful morning like him.

PROFESSOR. Yes. Yes. Of course. This magic morn. The wild green time is upon us. Summer is begun! (*Beat.*) Well, I best be off, Mr Byron. I can't miss the floats.

JOHNNY. Take care, Professor. If you want my advice: stick to the cider, get some cake in you around four. Keep your trousers on, and if you break any bones, or piss yourself, it's over. Go home. There's always next year.

PROFESSOR. What about Mary?

JOHNNY. Don't worry. If I sees your Mary I'll send her home.

PROFESSOR. *Adieu*, Mr Byron. To the revels!

JOHNNY. To the revels, Professor!

PROFESSOR (*whistles*). Mary! Mary…! (*Whistles.*) Mary!

Exit the PROFESSOR. JOHNNY *watches him leave.*
GINGER *comes out with the bacon rolls.*

GINGER. It's all go in Flintock. Trestle tables. Hot-dog vans… Bunting. Bumper cars. Whirler-swirler. Floats are all lined up in Garner's Field. There's a *Lord of the Rings* float, kids done up as hobbits, orcs… whatnot… fuckin' what's-his-name. Randolph.

JOHNNY. Gandalf.

GINGER. That's the one. There's a George and the Dragon. *Men in Black II*. Crown and Goose have gone *X Factor*. Same as last year. I say, make a bloody effort. Although old Roger Pyle done up as Sharon Osbourne is genuinely unsettling.

JOHNNY. Where's my money then?

GINGER. Tough. I'd say fifty-fifty between the birds from the gym as St Trinian's. Stockings. Suzzies. Whole shooting match. Bloody lush… And the lads from the rugby club all

turned out as golliwogs. Steel drums. Frizzy hair. Bit
offensive, but it's all for charity. Then. Right. In that field,
right, behind the graveyard, they've got, wait for it, 'A
Healing Experience'. They've got a 'Meditation Cave',
which is basically a polytunnel, and a massage tent. I am not
joking. You go in and Pat Cannon is sat in there alone on a
foldy chair, smoking a Lambert and Butler. I'm sorry but
not-fucking-likely am I going to pay ten quid to lie in the
dark and let Phil Cannon's mum get a cheapy. I've gone,
'Where's the massager, Pat?' 'I've fucking trained for six
months, you cheeky cunt. And anyway, it's *masseuse*.' So I
said, 'What's wrong with yer shoes?' (*Laughs.*) I tell you.
I'm on fire today. Stop me before I kill again.

GINGER *lets off the horn. A young man,* LEE, *suddenly sits
up from the couch, gasping.*

LEE. Mother!

JOHNNY. Morning, Lee.

GINGER. Bastard! You said he weren't here.

LEE. Where the fuck am I? Ow. My head.

GINGER. 'Gathering.' 'Gathering', mind.

JOHNNY. Cup of tea, Lee?

LEE. Lovely. That a spliff?

JOHNNY. What's it look like?

LEE. Lush. Morning, Ginger. You missed a classic last night, son.
Everyone was here. Didn't get cracking till after hours. Whizz.
Wangers. Sick beats. Tasty birds. Rum'n'Ribena. Benilyn
'n'brandy... Birds are going bats for it. Banging it back. Then,
right. Then. Right. Then. (*He cracks up.*) Then. Right. Then.
(*Laughs.*) Then. Right. Rooster. Right. (*Cracks up. He says it.
He's laughing so hard, you can't understand it.*)

GINGER. What?

LEE. Then. Right. Then. Right. Then. Then. (*Tries again.*)

GINGER *looks to* JOHNNY *for help.*

JOHNNY. Sorry. I can't help you.

LEE. Then. Then. Right. Then.

LEE, *in fits of laughter, starts signalling for a pen.*

GINGER. 'Gathering.' 'Gathering', mind…

LEE. Rooster brings his telly out and crowds everyone round and smashes it up with a cricket bat. (*Collapses laughing.*)

JOHNNY. No I never.

LEE *affirms that he did, laughing. We can't understand the words.*

Bollocks.

LEE (*still laughing, pointing, trying to say*). It's over there, mate.

They look over at a ruined pile of plastic, glass and circuitry, yonder.

JOHNNY. I never done that. I'd never do that.

LEE (*wiping tears from his eyes*). You had to be there, Ginger. It was unmissable.

GINGER (*to* LEE). Aren't you supposed to be gone?

LEE. Tomorrow, mate. Heathrow Airport. 6 a.m. coach from Chippenham.

GINGER. I thought it was today.

LEE. No fear. I'm hardly gonna sweat bullets for six months just to miss my last one. This is it, my lovers. Lee Piper's Last Flintock Fair.

JOHNNY. I shouldn't worry, boy. You'll be back next year.

LEE (*takes the ticket out of his pocket*). Check the ticket. One way, mate. I cleared out my room. Put all my old stuff on eBay. My old toys. Games. Posters. CDs.

GINGER. What you make?

LEE. Nothing. Not one bid. Action Man Utility Vehicle. Set of Smurfs. Life-size cardboard cut-out of Chewbacca. In the end, I put everything in six bin bags, lugs it up Oxfam. Old lady tells me to fuck off. So I lugs it back home and burned it in the garden.

GINGER. Nice. Final.

LEE. Fuck it. Can't take it with you.

JOHNNY. You can't now.

LEE. I got one haversack standing in Mum's hall. And two hundred Australian dollars. That's me.

JOHNNY. How long's that last? A week?

LEE. Duck and dive, mate. Watch the pennies. Plus, right. I'm on a fast.

JOHNNY. A what?

LEE. Fast. I'm purging myself.

JOHNNY. Why the fuck are you on a fast?

LEE. To clean out the system. Hone my willpower. Been going two weeks now. I was on Google buying my ticket, I found this link to this wicked site about the Potawatomies.

JOHNNY. The who?

LEE. Potawatomies. The Potawatomies are this double-hard Red Indian tribe. They ruled the Black Mountains of Dakota and terrorised the Bozeman Trail from 1851 to the late 1890s.

GINGER. Can't you just download porn like any sane human being?

LEE. Before a great journey, the Potawatomie braves used to go on fasts to gain knowledge. Build willpower. Vision quests. You go on a dreamquest and discover your true name. Your spirit name.

GINGER. So what's your Red Indian spirit name then, Lee?

JOHNNY. 'Burns His Smurfs.'

GINGER. 'Flies to Australia Then Comes Straight Back.'

LEE. You can take the piss. I learned loads. So I thought I'd give it a blast. I'm just purging myself. Preparing myself, thassall.

JOHNNY. What for?

LEE. The journey. What lies ahead. Come Monday, boy, all this is gone. Memories. From the other side of the world.

He takes the spliff, has a big wheeze. Holds it in. Enter DAVEY, *in big shades, with an accordion.*

DAVEY.
    Oh, where is St George,
    Oh, where is he-o?

ALL.
    He's out on his long boat,
    All on the sea-o!

DAVEY. Whassup, Ginger. Missed a classic last night, mate. Best one in weeks… Where was you?

GINGER. Last night. Let's see. I was up Ibiza. Celebrity booking at Pacha… Paid me ten thousand Europes. Hang on, last night. No, last night. I was sat at home in my Y-fronts watching telly. Pot Noodle. Unsuccessful wank. Bed. You lost my number then? Send me a text next time…

JOHNNY. Where've you been?

DAVEY. Over there. Dancing with these amazing trees.

JOHNNY. You playing today, Davey?

DAVEY. I'm on the Young Farmers' float. Then I'm at the Maypole. I haven't picked this up since last year, but it all comes back once you're mashed. (*Plays a bit. Stops. Sniffs.*) I'm sure someone's pissed in this accordion. That a spliff?

LEE. What's it look like?

DAVEY. Lush. Aren't you supposed to be gone?

LEE. 6 a.m., mate. Bus from Chippenham.

DAVEY. Rather you than me, mate. I've never seen the point of other countries. I leave Wiltshire, my ears pop. Seriously. I'm on my bike, pedalling along, see a sign says 'Welcome to Berkshire', I turn straight round. I don't like to go east of Wootton Bassett. Suddenly it's Reading, then London, then before you know where you are you're in France, and then there's just countries popping up all over. What's that about? I can't help it if I like it here. I can't help it if I'm happy. Here, Rooster. Who are your mates?

JOHNNY. What mates?

DAVEY. Bloke and a bird coming through the wood. Suits. Clipboards.

JOHNNY. Oh, them. Them's MI6. They want to know if I'll join the Cabinet. I told them to fuck off, I'm busy today.

GINGER *is looking at the notice on the door.*

GINGER. What's this?

JOHNNY. Don't you touch that. That's my bog paper, that. I shall be wiping my arse on that shortly so I don't want your grubby dabs all over it...

GINGER. Looks serious. Says 'Kennet and Avon Council' on the top. With numbers. And a seal.

JOHNNY. I ain't scared of Kennet and Avon. I been running rings round that lot since before you were born. There's council officials ten years dead, wake up in cold wet graves hollering the name of Rooster Byron. I'm in their dreams and their worst nightmares. Besides. My lawyers in New York deal with all that. Here, Davey? Did you smash my telly up?

DAVEY. No, son. You did. With a cricket bat.

JOHNNY. Bollocks.

DAVEY. You should have been there, Ginge. It was fucking hysterical.

GINGER. You're right. I should have.

JOHNNY. Bollocks. That's a brand-new telly.

DAVEY. You wanna see it. Hang about. I've got it here.

He takes out his phone. Squints.

Here, you do it. My eyes don't work.

He chucks it to LEE. JOHNNY *walks over.*

LEE. Here we go. How do you do the… / Here we go.

DAVEY (*overlapping*). Press the thing. The / fuckin'…

LEE (*overlapping*). How old is this?

DAVEY. The middle button. The thing –

LEE. Here we go.

They all stand round the phone. Sounds of music. Shouting.

GINGER. 'Gathering.' 'Gathering', mind.

JOHNNY. All right, Ginger, drop it.

GINGER. It's rammed. There's birds there I don't even know. Hang about. That's Rosie. That's my fucking little sister Rosie.

JOHNNY (*watches*). Who's that?

LEE. That's you.

JOHNNY. That's not me. There's no way that's me. What's that?

LEE. That's a cricket bat.

JOHNNY. Hang about. What is he doing? What's he doing?

PHONE RECORDING OF JOHNNY. Stand back, you vermin. Make room.

*Cheers: 'Five, four, three, two, one!' Sound of a man
smashing up his TV with a cricket bat. As the cheers ring out,*
JOHNNY *winces with every blow. He hands the phone back
and goes over to pick among the wreckage.*

JOHNNY (*shaking his head*). Well. That is a *complete* mystery.

LEE. That seemed a lot funnier last night.

DAVEY. It did. You had to be there. (*He plays a chord or two.*)

LEE. You're right, mate. Someone has pissed in that.

From beneath the trailer crawl two sixteen-year-old girls,
PEA *and* TANYA.

JOHNNY. Oi-oi. Fuck are you still doing here?

PEA. Where am I?

LEE. Morning, Pea. Tanya.

PEA. Morning, Lee. What time is it?

JOHNNY. Fuckin' kids is like rats. Crawling out of the
woodwork. Can't get rid of the bastards...

TANYA. Morning, Ginger. You missed one last night.

GINGER. For fuck's sake.

TANYA. Fucking immense. Non-stop, front-to-back, A1 class.

PEA. Hang about, Tanya. You've rolled in something.

TANYA. Where?

PEA. All up your back.

TANYA. What is it? Does it smell?

PEA. Fuck me...

TANYA. Is it in my hair?

DAVEY (*looks*). That's chicken, that.

LEE (*looks*). No it ain't. Chicken's runnier.

DAVEY. Trust me. That's chicken.

LEE. No way is that chicken. Chicken's greener. That is badger, mate. Possibly fox.

TANYA. Fuckin' 'ell, Rooster. This is a brand-new top.

JOHNNY. Turn round.

She does.

That's badger.

TANYA. Fuckin' 'ell.

JOHNNY. Serves you right. Why don't you fuck off home like the rest of 'em. Stop round Hayley's, you don't wanna go home…

JOHNNY *collects an axe from the porch. He goes over to a pile of logs to the side of the trailer. He takes one, puts it on a stump.*

LEE. Here, Tanya. You seen Phaedra?

TANYA. What?

LEE. Phaedra. Her mum said she ain't been home for days.

JOHNNY *splits a log.*

TANYA. I ain't seen her all week, mate.

PEA. Who's that?

LEE. Phaedra? She ain't been home.

PEA. Last time I saw Phaedra, right, was… fancy-dress night. Fancy-dress night at The 'Rakers.

TANYA. That doorman is a wanker.

GINGER. Why?

TANYA. He is. He's such a tuss.

GINGER. What happened?

PEA. She'd made her own costume, right, made a real effort, stitching, sequins, and she shows up at The 'Rakers and the fucking doorman turns her away.

LEE. Wanker.

GINGER. Why?

TANYA. He knows her stepdad. He knows she's fifteen.

LEE. Half the girls in there are fifteen.

JOHNNY *splits a log.*

PEA. 'Sorry, love. You're underage. Hop it.' She bursts into tears. Just runs off into the night.

LEE. Bastard.

PEA. Just walks off. No one's seen her since.

TANYA. She's always going off. Once, right, she had a fight with her mum, she went straight up the dual carriageway, fourteen years old.

DAVEY. You know what I reckon. I reckon she's been got by a werewolf. She's been turned away from The 'Rakers, wandered off into the night, in tears, whereupon a werewolf has heard her tragic sobs, and he's followed her through the brush and he's pounced. He's torn her arms and legs off and eaten her virgin heart. Seriously. In a day or two, someone'll find a bloody patch of turf in a clearing, with just these pink fairy wings flapping in the breeze.

PEA. Ugghh, gross.

LEE. Don't say that. That's awful.

DAVEY (*gives a demonic laugh*). 'I am the Flintock werewolf. I break not the branches as I step along.' (*Laughs.*)

LEE. I said shut up.

JOHNNY *splits a log.*

GINGER. Why you care so much about Phaedra Cox all of a sudden?

DAVEY. Yeah. You're leaving tomorrow. Left that one a bit late, mate.

LEE. No reason. (*Beat.*) What? Fuck off. I just want to say goodbye, that's all. You know. To everyone. Like… one for the road and that.

GINGER. 'One for the road.'

LEE. I didn't mean it like that.

TANYA. I'll give you one for the road, mate.

LEE. I didn't mean it like that.

TANYA. I did. Obviously not now. Later. When I'm not, like, you know…

PEA. Plastered in shit.

TANYA. Exactly. Once I'm not plastered in badger shit, obviously.

LEE. Cheers, mate. I'm good.

TANYA. Worth a try.

DAVEY. Squeaky wheel, mate. Squeaky wheel.

PEA. She'll show up today. Phaedra Cox is the May Queen.

DAVEY. What?

PEA. She won last year. Reigning May Queen has to crown the new Queen. If she don't show up, Flintock's got no Queen. She'll turn up. She has to. She's Queen of the Fair.

JOHNNY *splits a log. Gathers up the pieces to carry inside.*

JOHNNY. Right, you lot. Hear ye, 'cause I just passed a new law. From this day hence, take note that none of you rats is to kip over without written permission from my lawyers. I've had enough. If you can't stand up, piss off home. Any one caught breaking that law shall be strung up by their heels from the highest beech, until them's daft head pops. Hark ye. Johnny Byron has spoken.

He goes inside. GINGER *is looking at the notice on the door again.*

LEE. That Kennet and Avon?

PEA. Who's got the hump now?

GINGER. It's the New Estate.

LEE. They've got a petition up. It's gone to court. They've had powwow in the village hall and everything. A crisis meeting.

PEA. 'Crisis meeting'?

LEE. That's what I heard. It's all kicked off…

DAVEY. They've got a point, though, haven't they? I'm not being funny, right, but if you're sat in your brand-new house you've sweat your bollocks off to buy, and find out four hundred yards away there's some ogre living in a wood… I bet it never said in the brochure: 'Detached house, three beds with garden overlooking wood with free troll. Free ogre what loves trance music, deals cheap spliff and whizz, don't pay no tax, and has probably got AIDS. Guaranteed non-stop aggravation and danger.' I bet that weren't in the brochure.

LEE. He was going wild last night. Banging it back like it was going out of fashion. I don't know where he puts it.

DAVEY. Rooster's been giving it long-handle since Christmas. Longer.

TANYA. Last year at the fair. Watching him traipse round with that daft hat on. Pissed out his mind.

PEA. When he fell off the stage he was bleeding all down his back. Honestly. I was well embarrassed.

LEE. I dread to think what he's got planned today.

GINGER. Weren't always like that. Twenty year back, Johnny Byron *was* the Flintock Fair.

LEE. What d'you mean?

GINGER. People came from Berkshire. Dorset. Somerset, just
to see him.

LEE. Do what?

PEA. Get his bollocks out.

TANYA. Try and shag your mums?

GINGER. He was a daredevil. Used to jump buses on a trials
bike. All over Wiltshire. Dorset. The Downs. He jumped the
lot. Buses, tanks. Horseboxes. Jumped an aqueduct once. He
was gonna jump Stonehenge but the council put a stop to it.

LEE. And the rest.

GINGER. Local celebrity, mate. Flintock Fair, 1978, he jumped
thirteen buses.

PEA. Was they double-deckers?

TANYA. I bet they weren't. I bet they was Busy Bees.

GINGER. They never had Busy Bees back then. They'd be
double-deckers all right. May Days. Open Days. Agricultural
shows. Salisbury. Taunton. Bournemouth. Bath. Broke every
bone in his body. Broke his back in Swindon. Both arms in
Calne. His legs in Devizes. His neck in Newbury. Then, at
the Flintock Fair, 1981, he died.

LEE. What?

GINGER. He tried to jump twenty eighteen-wheelers, and he
fucked it up, and he died.

LEE. Bollocks.

GINGER. Mate, I was there. I saw it with my own eyes. He was
jumping all these eighteen-wheelers over in Stroyer's Farm.
Two thousand people at least. It was chucking it down and he
skidded on the ramp and flies through the air and he hits this
one truck doing about eighty mile an hour. He cartwheels
across the field like a rag doll and lies stone still. St John's
Ambulance ton it over. 'Stand clear.' Heart massage. Mouth-

to-mouth. He's dead. They pronounce him stone dead. St John's put a blanket over him. Paperwork, everything. All the mums are crying, how they should build a statue to him in the town square, when suddenly everyone turns round and he's gone. He's vanished. There's just a blanket with nothing under it. They follow this trail of blood across the field, past the whirler-swirler, into the beer tent, up to the bar, where he's stood there finishing a pint of Tally-Ho.

DAVEY. Bollocks.

GINGER. On my life. He just gone teethfirst into a lorry doing a hundred mile an hour, bounced twenty-five times, got one broken leg, one broken arm, broken jaw, no teeth, compressed spine, on top of which he's just spent ten minutes in the hereafter, and he gets up and hobbles in that tent, pays for his pint – 'Keep the change, love' – and downs it in one. Walks out. Walks it off.

LEE. I reckon that deserves a statue.

DAVEY. Fuck me.

LEE. Seriously. What did King Arthur ever do to top that?

PEA. So why'd he stop then?

GINGER. Council stepped in. Made daredevilling illegal. Come '91, '92, main attraction on Fair Day's some twat in a tent doing snooker trick-shots. Balloon animals. Smarty fucking arty.

LEE. The fucking fair's shit now.

DAVEY. It's shit.

LEE. It is. It's shit on toast.

DAVEY. Each year, right, everyone gets all excited, and each year it's that on toast.

GINGER. When I was a boy there was this big fucking farmer, right, and you paid ten pence to take a run-up and hoof him in the bollocks. If you brung him to his knees, you won a pound.

LEE. Simple. Pure.

GINGER. There was a queue about half a mile long. Kids.
Mums. Dads. All for charity.

LEE. Now that, my friends, is an attraction. That is
entertainment. What have they got now?

PEA. Throw a sponge at the lady vicar.

LEE. Guess the weight of the poorly hamster.

TANYA. They should put him in the town square. Next to King
Arthur.

PEA. His arm round King Arthur and a fucking great spliff on
the go.

LEE. 'Johnny Byron. Wiltshire's Biggest Bullshitter.'

JOHNNY *comes back out.*

Here, Johnny. They had a meeting about you. In the village
hall. Crisis meeting.

JOHNNY. What crisis meeting? What are you talking about?

LEE. The Johnny Byron Crisis Meeting. In the village hall.

JOHNNY. Oh, that.

LEE. You know about it.

JOHNNY. Yeah, I know about it. Actually – (*Belches.*) I went
to it.

LEE. What?

GINGER. What?

JOHNNY. I went along. I weren't busy, so I snuck in the back in
disguise. You get a cup of tea. Flapjack. Then they all sit
down on foldy chairs and go beserk. All these normal-
looking people screaming like banshees. Snakes on their
neck. Weeping with rage. Tearing their hair out. Everyone
gets very red in the face. This one mum, Kelly Wetherley,

she's up there, red in the face, microphone, saying, 'Johnny Byron is a filthy menace, Johnny Byron is a disgrace to Flintock,' and I swear to Christ I was shagging her only last June. I painted her house. Every time her husband went away she suddenly wanted her skirting boards seeing to. Stairs. Bedroom ceiling. In fact I'd say I know her pretty well, and I'm here to tell you, she goes a lot redder in the face than what she did at that meeting. That bedroom must've got sixteen coats. I counted five or six others sprinkled round that hall. I can't help it if they can't forget me. You watch. Four hundred yards down there, through them trees, across the brook, are seventy-eight brand-new houses. Them houses is lovely, clean and spanking now. But come two, three summers, couple hard winters, those windows'll peel. Doors. Ceilings. Skirting boards. Sooner or later those houses, trust me, those houses'll need painting.

There is a jingling in the wood.

LEE. What the fuck is that?

Enter WESLEY, *dressed as a morris dancer.*

WESLEY. Morning, Rooster.

JOHNNY. Wesley.

WESLEY. Morning, Lee. Ginger. Morning, all. Lovely morning. Listen, Rooster, I can't stay but I need a quick word.

JOHNNY. What the fuck's going on, Wesley?

WESLEY. Excuse me?

GINGER. Wesley. What are you wearing, mate?

WESLEY. Oh. Right. This. Right. (*Beat.*) Basically. Don't go there. Basically, it's a long story. First of all. It weren't my idea. Secondly, fuck off, okay? I know. Whatever. So. Yes. Basically. I got roped in.

JOHNNY. Roped in to what?

WESLEY. We're doing a round outside The Cooper's this afternoon.

JOHNNY. Who's 'we'?

WESLEY. Me and the lads. For the fair.

GINGER. You and the who?

WESLEY. The boys. The lads. The Flintock Men.

ALL. Who the fuck are the Flintock Men?

WESLEY. It's a long story. Got roped in to it really. It's the brewery's idea. They twisted my arm.

LEE. How long you been doing it?

WESLEY. Six weeks.

LEE. How long's the Flintock Men been going?

WESLEY. Six weeks. But it's not all doom and gloom. I'm the Barley Sword Bearer.

TANYA. Who?

PEA. The what?

WESLEY. The Barley Sword Bearer. They have this big cake with loads of bottles of brandy, Tia Maria, advocaat, whatever they can't shift, all that in it. I cut the cake and distribute it among the womenfolk. It's bollocks, really. Basically it connotes fertility and the hunt.

GINGER. And you're comfortable with this?

WESLEY. It's the brewery's idea. They've got right behind the fair this year. Point-of-sale material. T-shirts. Flintock Men. Special ale.

JOHNNY. Can't you just tell 'em to fuck off. Tell 'em it's your pub.

WESLEY. It's a Swindon-level decision. Even if I wanted to, it's out of my hands.

JOHNNY. It's wrong, Wesley. Something is deeply wrong.

WESLEY. Look, Johnny, I need to speak to you.

JOHNNY. And I need to speak to you, mate. Why you ban me from The Cooper's? If it's about the fracas then that whole incident is a tissue of hearsay and insinuations. If you choose to ban me that's a diabolical liberty bordering on the criminal and I will put my lawyers onto it and fight it with every ounce of my –

WESLEY. It's not about the fracas. It ain't about that. It's private.

Pause. The others look at each other. Sense it's time to say –

LEE. Right. I'm off.

DAVEY. Yeah, I better make tracks. I said I'd help Mum set up the tombola.

TANYA. I gotta change.

PEA. Me too. I'm doing the donkey drop.

DAVEY. Fuck's a donkey drop?

GINGER. As I understand it – with a donkey drop, you stake out a patch a grass in squares, walk a donkey round, if it craps in your square, you win a prize.

PEA. We're doing it out by the standing stones. Then I'm on the *Men in Black II* float 'bout two. What time you dancing, Wesley?

WESLEY. On an' off all bloody day.

PEA. Might see you on the Wheelbeero Race. Can't really miss a load of pissed morris dancers.

GINGER. Yeah, I better get over there too. I gotta prepare.

LEE. What for? What you doing?

GINGER. I gotta prepare my set today.

PEA. What set? What you on about?

GINGER. I'm DJing.

JOHNNY. No he's not.

GINGER. Yes I am.

JOHNNY. He's not.

GINGER. I fucking am. Possibly. I'm standby DJ at The Cooper's.

WESLEY. Are you?

GINGER. Yes I fucking am. I spoke to Sue.

WESLEY. She never said nothing. When?

GINGER. Last week. I'm back-up for 2 Trevs. If the 2 Trevs can't make it, or, say, one or both of the Trevs is ill.

WESLEY. I just spoke to them, they're fine. They're on their way.

GINGER. Right. But, what if they, you know…

LEE. Get lost?

DAVEY. Crash?

LEE. Have a fight. Musical differences.

GINGER. Or food poisoning. One of them could eat a dodgy burger.

LEE. They're called 2 Trevs. There's two Trevs. So if one Trev eats a dodgy burger. There's a spare Trev.

WESLEY. I'll suggest they eat different meals.

DAVEY. They're not landing a fucking 747. They're playing Chumbawumba in a pub car park.

PEA (*kisses* JOHNNY *on the cheek*). Thanks for the party, Johnny. And for letting us stop over.

TANYA. Under.

JOHNNY. Not that you asked. Cheeky moo.

PEA. You wouldn't have let us.

JOHNNY. Too bloody right.

TANYA. Catch you later, lover.

They leave.

LEE. Where you gonna be for the Spitfire flyby?

GINGER. Parker's Field? Maybe Orr Hill.

LEE. Sweet. Text me. Laters, Ginger. Laters, Wesley.

DAVEY *nudges* LEE.

Right. Uh. Johnny, can I have a quick word?

JOHNNY. Fuck off.

LEE. What? What did I say?

JOHNNY. The answer's no.

LEE. Just a cheeky gram.

JOHNNY. Fiver.

LEE. Chalk it up.

JOHNNY. You're *emigrating* tomorrow.

LEE. Come on, mate, it's my last fair. I done my nuts on the flight. Chalk us one up. For Auld Lang Syne.

JOHNNY. I ain't got no chalk.

DAVEY. It's all in the whizz…

JOHNNY. You snafflers weren't griping last night.

LEE. Come on. It's St George's Day. Lend us a bluey, Davey.

DAVEY. I'm out.

LEE. Ginge?

GINGER. See, Lee, what we have here is what you might call a parable.

JOHNNY. I got pockets full of promises off you chisellers. 'Lend us a tenner, Rooster.' 'I'll pays you later, Roost.' 'Here's a DVD of *Top Gun. Remains of the* fucking *Day*.' There has to be rules. Two weeks back, your brother Daffy comes round here, tries to buy three grams of whizz with a tortoise.

LEE. That weren't his tortoise. That's my sister's tortoise.

JOHNNY. Well, now it's my fucking tortoise. Little bugger pisses everywhere. It pisses pints. It's like the TARDIS.

LEE. He's right. That tortoise pisses like a shirehorse.

DAVEY. All right. Here's the portfolio. Ginger buys a gram, we go halves. When I get paid I give him a bluey. He gets half a wrap and a bluey, or one and a half wraps for the price of one. Johnny gets a tenner. Life goes on.

LEE. What do I get?

DAVEY. Keep out of this. You're broke.

LEE. Okay. Johnny. You lend us a fiver. I give it to Ginge, he buys a wrap. We split that, when I get to Australia, I post Ginge the fiver, he runs it round to you, you give him a wrap, he sells it to Davey who posts me back a fiver and I pays you back.

DAVEY. Sounds fair.

LEE. How's that.

JOHNNY. It's just that type of thinking what sunk this economy. Seriously. This is how it happened.

GINGER. It's not very green neither. Time you're finished, that wrap'll have a carbon footprint like a fucking yeti…

DAVEY. Come on, Johnny. It's the fair. Fair needs a sparkle.

LEE. It's shit when you're slotted. Imagine how bad it really is.

DAVEY. Don't put us through that. Have a heart.

WESLEY. Johnny –

JOHNNY. No IOUs. No bartering. No favours nor tick nor never-bloody-never. Fair or no fair. Turn out your pockets. If all you find's a hanky – hop it, soppy bollocks. I ain't Save the Children.

JOHNNY reaches into his jacket.

Here, Lee. Give this to your sister.

He hands him a tortoise.

LEE. Ah. Thanks, mate.

He considers offering it straight back. Then offers it to GINGER.

Ginger. Quick tortoise. Two careful owners…?

GINGER. I'm good, mate.

LEE. Laters.

LEE and DAVEY leave.

GINGER. Cup of tea, Wesley?

WESLEY. Lovely.

GINGER goes inside. JOHNNY pours himself another drink.

JOHNNY. Bloody kids. Like rats. Can't get rid of the bastards. Listen. I know Sue's got the hump with me, but –

WESLEY. What's going on, Johnny?

JOHNNY (*sings Marvin Gaye*). 'Come on, talk to me… and you can see – what's going on, what's on… I'll tell you what's going on…'

WESLEY. Don't give me that. What's going on?

JOHNNY. Is correct. You named that tune in four…

WESLEY. What you doing?

JOHNNY. What? Where?

WESLEY. Here.

JOHNNY. Where?

WESLEY. Here. What's that about?

JOHNNY. Oh, that. Knees-up last night. You know kids. Like trying to get stink off shit.

WESLEY. They're sleeping here?

JOHNNY. What would you rather they do, sat round in the bus shelter on the gas? Least it's warm here.

WESLEY. Tanya Crawley's sixteen years old.

JOHNNY. What's your point, caller?

WESLEY. Nothing. What? Nothing. Just…

JOHNNY. She was pissed last night. Can't have kids wandering around at night pissed. I never even knew she was fuckin' there. So what's your point, caller?

Beat.

WESLEY. Johnny, Listen. Phaedra Cox has gone off again. She ain't been home since Monday night.

JOHNNY. So?

WESLEY. So, I know she comes up here. With the others. Have you seen her?

JOHNNY. You know me, Wesley. I can't tell these rats apart.

WESLEY. It's not funny, Johnny. She's fifteen years old. Troy Whitworth was in the pub. In the saloon bar, asking if anyone had seen her.

JOHNNY. Phaedra Cox ain't my lookout. She's him's. She's Troy Whitworth's. He's her stepdad. Not me.

WESLEY. I just wondered if you seen her, is all. It's just…

JOHNNY. Just what?

WESLEY. Nothing. What? Come on, Johnny. You know what.

JOHNNY. I ain't seen her. Phaedra Cox ain't none of my
business.

WESLEY. It's just –

JOHNNY. I said I ain't seen her, Wesley.

WESLEY. Good. Good. Well, that's what I thought. (*Beat.*)
Come on, Johnny. You got kids here day and night, Johnny.
Look at all this. They're drinking.

JOHNNY. They're fifteen-, sixteen-year-old kids. Course
they're bloody drinking. It's not like you don't serve kids.
Bloody What's-it's Stringer, sat at the bar, he's fourteen year
old. Orderin' Maker's Mark and Coke. We had a lock-in the
night he was born. You get 'em straight off the climbing
frame and in the bloody snug.

WESLEY. That's different.

JOHNNY. What's different about it? How much you make a
week off the Breezers? Vodka Red Bulls? Goes like this:
Kids love drinking. Always did. They either sit in the bus
stop, shivering their bollocks off, or they go to yours, or they
come here. Everyone knows what they're up to, all the mums
and dads. Why? Because they did the same fuckin' thing, and
younger. There's not one mum or dad round here could come
here and say they weren't drinking, smoking, pilling and the
rest when they was that and younger. And shagging too. Like
cats in a sack.

WESLEY. Oh, bloody hell.

JOHNNY. How old were you when you lost your pip?

WESLEY. I don't know.

JOHNNY. Go on. How old?

WESLEY. Look. I can't recall.

JOHNNY. I can. You was twelve.

WESLEY. Bollocks.

JOHNNY. You was twelve years old. I should know, I was there. Flintock Fair, nineteen-bloody-sixty-whatever. Stone barn, out by Wilcot Poplars.

WESLEY. Okay, Johnny.

JOHNNY. On an orange tarpaulin. With fifty cows watching.

WESLEY. I know, it's just…

JOHNNY. Just what?

WESLEY. It was my first time. I don't like to think of you there.

JOHNNY. Well, I was there. And I was losing my pip. We was all losing our pips. What was she called? Heather something.

WESLEY. Heather Bloom.

JOHNNY. Heather Bloom.

WESLEY. Lovely soft skin. Alice Witherspoon.

JOHNNY. Had her 'n all.

WESLEY. Everyone had her. Witherspoon.

JOHNNY. With anything you fancied…

WESLEY. She was bloody lush.

JOHNNY. Flintock Fair Queen, 1969. Sweet fifteen. Apple of town's eye. Little did they know she'd laid on more balls than David Beckham.

WESLEY. Christ. The Flintock Fair. Summer of Love, though.

JOHNNY. Was for us.

They remember.

WESLEY. Look, fuck it. Sue'll kill me, but fuck it. Sue's brother Jim's in the South Wiltshire. He's in the pub this morning at the bar with two more off-duty. I'm bottling up, earwigging, one of them leans in, says, 'South Wiltshire have got that bastard Byron cornered.' It's gone through Salisbury Court. A court order. That, 9 a.m. tomorrow, they're togging up with shields, batons, dogs, they're gonna flush that bastard Byron out his hole. They been planning it for ten weeks. It's signed off.

Pause.

JOHNNY. It's signed off.

WESLEY. All right. Mate. Whatever. I done my bit. I'm just an earwig.

JOHNNY. Is that what you are?

WESLEY. Wake up, Johnny. What's that on your door?

JOHNNY. Looks like a piece of paper, Wesley.

WESLEY. 'Piece of paper.' 'Piece of paper.'

JOHNNY. Them's Kennet and Avon, love-writing to me. I get love letters every day.

WESLEY. 'Love letter.' 'Piece of paper.'

He reads the notice on the door.

Here. 'Piece of paper.' Listen. (*Reads.*) Kennet and Avon Council Injunction F-99. Salisbury Magistrates' Court rules that aforementioned Mr Byron shall be forthwith and forcibly evicted by Kennet and Avon Council bailiffs in cooperation with South Wiltshire Constabulary at 9 a.m., Saturday 24th April.

JOHNNY. How long have you known me, Wesley? Do you think the South Wiltshire, the dim-dumb brick-brained sausage-fingered South Wiltshire Police Force are planning something for ten weeks and I don't know about it? I have eyes everywhere, Wesley. Plain-clothes drives down Flintock High Street, round the roundabout, circles back, you think I don't clock that? A binocular flash out there through the trees? You can't get the daylight past the Rooster.

Beat.

WESLEY. What are you going to do?

Beat.

JOHNNY. You tell Sue's brother Jim to tell all his South Wiltshire bandits and all them fuckers on the New Estate that this wood is called Rooster's Wood. I've been here since before all you bent busybody bastards were born. I'm heavy stone, me. You try and pick me up, I'll break your spine.

Pause.

Have a good one, Wesley.

WESLEY. All right, mate. I'll catch you later.

He turns and leaves.

JOHNNY. Oh, and Wesley.

WESLEY *stops.*

WESLEY. Yes, mate.

Pause.

JOHNNY. Pinch Sue's bum from me.

WESLEY *exits.* JOHNNY *is alone. From the village we hear drums and singing:*

VOICES.
With the merry ring, adieu the merry spring,
For summer is a-come unto day,
How happy is the little bird that merrily doth sing,
In the merry morning of May.

Unite and unite,
For summer is a-come unto day,
And wither we are going we all unite,
In the merry morning of May!

JOHNNY *walks to his front door. He takes the notice off the door. He walks out into the light and examines it.*

Enter GINGER *with a programme for the fair.*

GINGER (*opens the programme*). Ladies and gentleman, I give you… The Annual St George's Day Pageant and Wessex Country Fair in the Village of Flintock sponsored by John Deere Tractors and Arkell Ales. (*Flicks through.*) Introduction from the Mayor… Blah blah blah. Picture of him and his fat missus. Here we go. 10 a.m., The Flintock Men – outside The Cooper's Arms. 11 a.m., Floats. 11.30, Ploughing competition. 11.45, Bell-ringing. 12 o'clock, Donkey drop. 12.15, Yoga demonstration. 12.30, Wheelbeero race. 12.45, Dancing dog display. 1 p.m., Knobbly knees. 1.15, Clowntown. Welly wanging, 1.30 –

JOHNNY. I ain't going.

Pause.

GINGER. What?

JOHNNY. I ain't going up the fair today.

GINGER. What's wrong? What happened?

JOHNNY *sets fire to the notice.*

He winds the siren defiantly. GINGER *stands and watches. Blackout.*

Curtain.

After any applause…

P.A. ANNOUNCEMENT. Ladies and gentlemen, welcome to the Annual St George's Day Flintock Fair. It's my distinct pleasure as wife to the Mayor to declare this day of festivities officially open.

Applause.

End of Act One.

PROLOGUE II

Spotlight. PHAEDRA *appears, again dressed as a fairy. She sings 'Werewolf' by Barry Dransfield.*

As she finishes, the curtain rises on...

ACT TWO

Heavy dub music. Two o'clock. On the side of the trailer is a big bedsheet stretched out which reads 'FUCK OFF KENNET AND AVON'. DAVEY *stands on the roof of the trailer with binoculars, sipping a beer, in a vest, as lookout.* LEE, *in shades, a spliff on the go and a butcher's apron, hoists the Jolly Roger over the trailer, before tending to the barbecue.*

Nearby, PEA *is carefully painting on the last letter to another bedsheet sign, which so far reads 'FUCK OFF THE NEW ESTAT'. On the porch,* GINGER *has his decks set up, headphones on, being cool, onstage in front of ten thousand people.*

Enter the PROFESSOR *from behind the caravan, sleeves rolled up, whistling, pushing a wheelbarrow full of gnomes.* LEE *directs him as to where to line them up. They discuss it briefly, and agree.* LEE *slaps him on the back.*

JOHNNY *comes out in his helmet and blows a whistle. Everyone stops what they're doing and he musters them in a line in the middle of the clearing.*

JOHNNY *hands a honey jar to* GINGER. *It has a big fat bee on it.* GINGER *unscrews the lid and goes along the line and pops a pill in everyone's mouth. On the end, with the* PROFESSOR, DAVEY *hands him a teacup. He drops it in, gives it a stir, and the* PROFESSOR *drinks it.*

As one, they all start to dance in unison. Towards the end of the song, LEE *sounds the submarine 'Dive! Dive! Dive!' and everyone gathers at the table.*

TANYA *comes out of the trailer with a tray of drinks. Everyone gets one. As one, they find their places at the table, drain their cups and bang them on the table.* JOHNNY *stands as the music stops, to cries of:*

ALL. Bollocks! Bollocks!

JOHNNY *raises his hands.*

JOHNNY. It's true. My mother was a virgin when she bore me!

ALL. Bollocks! Bollocks!

JOHNNY *raises his hands, on a roll.*

JOHNNY. See, my father, Hector Byron, was a philanderer. Loves the lasses. One May morning, he says, 'I'm off for a walk.' Now, his wife, who knows his ways of old, tracks the old goat's scent up the road, round the corner, straight up to the door of her own sweet sister. She crepples inside, up the stairs, into the boudoir, to find sister bent double on a big brass bed, with Hector up the back, in the cheap seats, whooping it up with all his lusty puff. The wife pulls a pistol, draws a bead and shoots the wayward lad slap-bang in the love bells. The bullet passes clean through his scrotum, bounces off the bedpost, zings out the window, down the high street to the crossroads, where it hits the number 87 tram to Andover. The bullet passes through two inches of rusty metal, clean through an elderly lady's packed lunch and lodges in my sweet mother's sixteen-year-old womb. Eight months, three weeks, six days later. Out pops him. Smiling. With a bullet clenched between his teeth.

GINGER. First of all. Babies don't have teeth.

JOHNNY. All Byron boys are born with teeth. Thirty-two chompers. And hair on them's chest. No wailing or weeping. Talkin', straight off. This one – me – he sits up, wipes the dew from his eyes and calls, 'Mother, what is this dark place?' And she replied, ''Tis England, my boy. England.' And with that, I jumps off the bed, and out the door, and off I marched in my little black cloak.

GINGER. Where did that come from?

JOHNNY. What?

GINGER. The cloak. Where did the cloak come from?

JOHNNY. All Byron boys come with their own cloaks. My brother Cyril's was red. Frank's was green. I'm born in black. With black eyes. You watch a black-cloaked Byron boy like a hawk, and tend him like a wound. You bind him, you swaddle him tight. And when they searched me –

GINGER. Wait. Stop. They searched you.

JOHNNY. Of course.

GINGER. Why did they search you?

JOHNNY. Always search a Byron boy at birth. You never know what he's got on him. A Byron boy comes with three things. A cloak and a dagger, and his own teeth. He comes fully equipped. He doesn't need nothing. And when he dies, he lies in the ground like a lump of granite. He don't rot. There's Byron boys buried all over this land, lying in the ground as fresh as the day they was planted. In them's cloaks. With the teeth sharp. Fingernails sharp. And the two black eyes, staring out, sharp as spears. You get close and stare into those black eyes, watch out. Written there is old words that will shake you. Shake you down.

GINGER. Let's get back to the bullet. Let's go back to the bit where you were born on the tip of a speeding bullet.

JOHNNY. You don't believe me.

He takes a bullet from his pocket. Tosses it to GINGER.

GINGER. Could be any old bullet.

He tosses it back.

JOHNNY. Any old bullet, eh? (*He puts it between his teeth.
Smiles.*) So there you have it. I am the only man in history to
be conceived in separate postal zones. Born one day early
and I've been a day ahead of all you beggars ever since. (*He
smiles.*)

ALL. Bollocks!

Bullshit!

JOHNNY *bangs the table.*

JOHNNY. Friends! Outcasts. Leeches. Undesirables. A blessing
on you, and upon this beggars' banquet. This day we draw a
line in the chalk, and push back hard against the bastard
pitiless busybody council, and drive them from this place for
ever. I, Rooster Byron, your merciless ruler, have decreed
that today all my bounty is bestowed upon you, gratis. There
will be free booze, bangers, draw, whizz and whatnot, for all
the minions of my kingdom.

Cheers from those gathered.

Before I begin, I want to say a few words about one here
who is leaving us. A son of this vale, born of this soil, he's
lived fair a score year among us, but tomorrow sets sail on a
voyage to the far side of the world.

Cheers.

And although we know he'll go broke inside a week, find
nothing but savages and end up selling his bum round Botany
Bay, he goes to his doom with our blessing. Lee Piper, you're
a pisshead, a whizzhead and you don't pay your way. But
you're the only one of these buggers I'd trust with a lit
match. So here's your blessing. Tanya.

TANYA *stands. Clears her throat.*

TANYA.
>May the road rise to meet you,
>May the wind be always at your back,
>May the sun shine warm upon your face,
>And the rains fall soft upon your fields,
>And, until we meet again,
>May God hold you in the palm of His hand.
>And if you want that free one, come back to my mum's,
>And I'll get you halfway to Australia for nothing.

They cheer. 'Speech! Speech! Speeeech!!' LEE stands. Raises a hand.

LEE. Thank you. Thank you, Tanya. Thank you to all. I've been very happy here and. Right. And. Right. And. Right. And. Right.

He starts to cry.

GINGER. Steady the bus.

DAVEY. Here we go.

GINGER. Come on, skipper. Keep the cable tight. Gather. Gather.

They all take the piss.

LEE. I'm all right. I'm fine. Relax. I'm back. Fuck off. Fuck off. I'm back. (*He holds a hand up.*) Rooster. You've proved today you're not just an old gyppo, tight as two coats of paint, a dangerous nutter they should put behind glass, chuck in a box and strap to the back of a diving blue whale. And even if you gets us all killed today, at least we'll all show up in Heaven pissed. Cheers!

Cheers.

PROFESSOR. Well, this is indeed a fitting scene. It is an Englishman's duty at the first scent of May to make the turf his floor, his roof the arcing firmament. And his clothes the leaves and branches of the glade.

JOHNNY. Hear, hear!

PROFESSOR. In 1521 when Henry VIII set forth with his
   young bride, Catherine of Aragon, and sat down upon the
   fields at Lambeth, he was continuing a tradition which
   already spanned back millennia. This is a time for revelry.

JOHNNY. Hear, hear!

PROFESSOR. To be free from constraint. A time to commune
   with the flora and the fauna of this enchanted isle. To
   abandon oneself to the rhythms of the earth.

ALL. Hear, hear!

LEE. Look at him. He's mad into it.

GINGER. It's a good job. In thirty minutes he's going to be
   dancing with his shirt round his head strapped to the front of
   the Starship Enterprise.

LEE. I shall look forward to that.

JOHNNY. Cohorts! Beloved spongers!

   Cheers.

   Make merry. For tonight, like a flaming flock of snakes, we
   will storm Flintock Village and burn every house, shop and
   farm. We will behead the Mayor. Imprison the Rotary Club.
   Pillage the pubs! Rob the tombola! And whip into a
   whirlwind a roughhead army of unwashed, unstable,
   unhinged, friendless, penniless, baffled berserkers what
   haunt that Godforsaken town, and together, snout by jowl,
   we will rise up and ride on Salisbury, Marlborough, Devizes,
   Calne, until the whole plain of Wiltshire dances to the tune
   of our misrule.

   Cheers.

   God damn the Kennet and Avon. Fuck the New Estate!

ALL. Hear, hear!

   Fuck the New Estate!

   Enter WESLEY.

WESLEY. Afternoon, all.

JOHNNY. It's the enemy! Our dastard foe!

ALL. Fuck off.

Away with you!

WESLEY. I see you're having fun then. Excellent. (*He looks at the sign.*) That's nice, Rooster. Very nice.

JOHNNY. You like that, do you, Wesley? Pea done that all by herself.

GINGER (*to* PEA). Don't you live on the New Estate?

PEA. Pendragon Close. Up the end.

WESLEY. Well, I'm just glad you're enjoying yourself. I'm glad to see you've taken our little chat to heart.

JOHNNY. Oh, I did, Wesley. I heard every word.

WESLEY. Splendid. Just so long as we all know what day it is today.

JOHNNY. This, Wesley, is a historic day. For today, I, Rooster Byron, and my band of educationally subnormal outcasts shall swoop and raze your poxy village to dust. In a thousand years, Englanders will awake this day and bow their heads and wonder at the genius, guts and guile of the Flintock Rebellion. Davey Dean will be on a ten-pence coin. Lee Piper will be on a plinth in Trafalgar Square. Tanya Crawley and Pea Gibbons will have West End musicals written for them by Andrew Lloyd Webber and Sir Elton John. The Professor will be hailed in the same breath as Sir Isaac Newton and Charles Darwin, and after all that, still no one will ever remember who the fuck was Ginger Yates.

GINGER. Thanks very much. Cheers. Whatever.

DAVEY. I say we torture him.

TANYA. Off with his head!

PEA. Burn him. Burn him alive! Rips his bells off!

JOHNNY. What do you say, Professor? Are we torturers?

PROFESSOR. Well, let's see. English rebellions by their very nature are generally bloodthirsty affairs. I suggest we might put his head on a pike. As a dire warning to the villagers.

JOHNNY. It's just that type of cold-blooded reasoning which will immortalise you, Professor.

ALL. Burn him! Burn him!

Off with his head!

WESLEY. Well, I'd love to oblige but the saloon bar's heaving. So I'll have to love you and leave you. I just popped over to catch young Lee before he flies. Lee, mate, Sue and I are sad that, come tomorrow, you won't be with us, so we all clubbed together and got you this.

He takes out a red T-shirt. It says:

'FARE
WELL
LEE?'

on the front.

LEE. Thanks, Wesley.

WESLEY. And Sue.

LEE. Thanks, Sue. Thanks, Sue and Wesley.

WESLEY. Sue devised the slogan. Slight snafu. That's actually an exclamation mark.

LEE. Right.

WESLEY. I've called the printers. They can turn it around in forty-eight hours. 'No, good chum,' said I. 'He'll be long gone.' If it helps, Sue is livid with me. Not happy at all. Anyway, we'll all miss you at The Cooper's. Bring us back a boomerang.

LEE. Thanks, Wesley. And Sue. I'm touched.

WESLEY. So.

JOHNNY. Is that it, Wesley? Is that all you wanted?

WESLEY. Yes. What? Yes. That's it. That's all. I just thought, you know… (*Beat.*) Look, it's just, it's Fair Day and I've gotta do this fucking dancing all day, and I'm knackered, see, from working all week. Just need a little buzz to get the party going. Come on, Johnny. Just get me through this palaver in one fucking piece. Sue's driving me mad. I'm dressed like a cunt. Come on, mate. Cut me some slack.

Pause.

JOHNNY. How much do you want?

WESLEY. Oh, cheers, mate. Just a cheeky gram'll do. Two if you can spare it.

JOHNNY. All right. I'll give you two gram. On one condition.

Pause.

WESLEY. No. (*Pause.*) No bloody way. (*Pause.*) No bloody way.

JOHNNY. No? Suit yourself.

WESLEY. I won't fucking do it.

GINGER. All day long without any whizz.

WESLEY. No.

JOHNNY. You know you wants to. You're gagging for it. You loves a bit of whizz. You *loves* it.

WESLEY. I won't do it.

LEE. Come on!

DAVEY. Go on, my son!

JOHNNY. Suit yourself.

ALL. WESLEY! WESLEY! WESLEY! WESLEY!

WESLEY. Three grams.

Everyone cheers.

JOHNNY. I want the goods up-front. And no skimping.

More chanting. He takes a deep breath, dances a round, with all the leaps and moves, lightly humming the music.

WESLEY. Fucking cunts. All right. So this is one. And… See, each dance you do, each one connotes a different thing.

He demonstrates.

JOHNNY. What does that connote?

GINGER. Yeah. What does that connote, Wesley.

JOHNNY. I'm no expert, but to me it says, 'I have completely lost my self-respect.'

LEE. 'I need to radically rethink my values.'

DAVEY. 'I will humiliate myself for poor-quality drugs.'

WESLEY. For your information, it connotes the sun god's mastery over the infinite chaos of the galaxy.

JOHNNY. I was just going to say that.

WESLEY. Happy now?

JOHNNY. It's in there on the breadboard. And enjoy it, mate, because it's your last. We'll be out here sharpening the axe.

WESLEY *goes inside.*

TANYA. Rooster. Is it true you was a daredevil? You jumped Stonehenge?

JOHNNY. Who told you that?

TANYA. Ginger.

GINGER. I never said that.

TANYA. He did, he said you was a daredevil and you jumped Stonehenge.

JOHNNY. You don't want to believe everything you hear, now, girls. There's some men'll tell you anything to get you to

believe it. I never jumped Stonehenge. But I once met a giant
that built Stonehenge.

GINGER. Oh, really. And where was that?

JOHNNY. Just off the A14 outside Upavon. About half a mile
from the Little Chef. I'd been up for three days and nights
straight, playing canasta with these old ladies in a retirement
home outside Wootton Bassett. They were extremely good
players. They bled me white. I didn't even have the money
left for half a gallon of two star to fill the bike to get me
home. So I set off from Wootton round midnight, and I ran
out of petrol outside Wilcot, three, four in the morning. It's a
good job too because after three nights drinking neat
Drambuie with nothing but custard creams to soak it up, I
was too fusky to ride it. So I pushes it through the night all
the way from Wilcot to Potterne. And coming down the hill
into the town, I peered over the hedge – squinted a bit, I was
a bit bleary, see – and there he was sitting on the bluff.
Gazing out over the land, watching the sun rise.

DAVEY. Hang on. When you say 'giant'. Do you mean big
bloke, or, like, giant. I mean, how tall was he?

JOHNNY. It's hard to say exactly because he was sitting down.
I'd have to guess. Maybe forty, forty-five feet seated. So
ninety, a hundred foot. Give or take.

GINGER. Ninety feet tall.

JOHNNY. Give or take. So I got off my bike and went over, and
we got to chatting.

GINGER. What did you chat about?

JOHNNY. This and that. The weather mostly.

GINGER. The weather.

JOHNNY. He thought it was going to be a dry summer. I
thought not. He said he'd walked from Land's End that very
morning, and there was sand on the beach at the Lizard. And
if there's sand on the Lizard 1st April, the summer'll be dry.

Turned out it was complete bollocks. He's was completely wrong. He didn't know what the fuck he was talking about. Rained clean through July and August. But in passing, he did mention he built Stonehenge.

GINGER. Stonehenge. He built Stonehenge.

JOHNNY. He didn't make no song and dance about it. He just pointed over yonder, said, 'See that over there. I done that.'

GINGER. 'I built Stonehenge.'

JOHNNY. That's if you believe him. It could be bullshit.

GINGER. Could it.

JOHNNY. I don't suppose there's any reason for him to make something like that up.

GINGER. Why would you? What's the fucking point?

JOHNNY. Then he said, 'Well, whatever's coming, this is one beautiful morning.' And he stood up, and he said, 'I've got something for you.' And he went to his right ear, and hanging from it was this golden drum. Big as a kettle drum. He said, 'This is for you. If you ever get in any bother, or you need a hand, just bang this drum and us, the giants, we'll hear it, and we'll come.' Then he headed off down the vale, and I watched him walk clean across the land, north towards the motorway, until he was off in the distance like a pylon.

GINGER. First of all. When you meet a *giant*. The clue is in the name. He's not an inconspicuous thing. If a ninety-foot giant walks from Land's End up to Salisbury Plain in the blazing spring sunshine, some cunt other than Johnny Byron is going to clock the cunt. It's at the very least going to be on BBC *Points West*. At the very least.

LEE. Good point.

GINGER. Trust me. If they put a burst drain at Alderbury first item up, they are going to put a ninety-foot-tall, three-thousand-year-old giant what says he built Stonehenge. They just are. Eh? Aren't they.

LEE. It's reasonable.

GINGER. They are. Aren't they.

LEE. I imagine they are, Ginge.

GINGER. Pea? Tanya?

PEA. Sounds about right.

TANYA. Never thought of that.

GINGER. Professor.

PROFESSOR. It's a good point.

GINGER. Davey.

DAVEY. I'm not so sure.

GINGER. What do you mean, you're not sure?

DAVEY. I mean, I'm in two minds.

GINGER. You seriously don't think that would make BBC *Points West*. A giant.

DAVEY. Who can say these days. You ask me, BBC *Points West* has lost its way.

GINGER. What?

DAVEY. *Points West* used to be solid local news. First they've done the cuts, merged with Bristol, now it's half the bloody country.

PROFESSOR. He's right, you know. In broadening its net it's saved on costs at the – some would say – greater cost at a level of editorial focus.

GINGER. You keep out of this.

DAVEY. I was watching this one story about this old lady, eighty-seven-year-old, these kids have jumped her in an alley and kicked her to death for her scratchcard.

PEA. I saw that.

PROFESSOR. I saw that. Terrible.

DAVEY. Right. And I'm at home, on me own, watching, getting that upset, tearing up, the lot, before I realise it's some old biddy from Wales. Some Welsh nonsense. Good luck to 'em. I ain't never even fucking been there and I never fucking will.

PROFESSOR. She was from Barry Island.

DAVEY. Exactly. I mean, who in their right minds gives a fuck?

PEA. Local is Bedwyn. Local is Devizes.

DAVEY. You want to gas yourself in your garage in Gloucester, be my guest. How could I possibly care less?

TANYA. Show me a good house fire in Salisbury. Now *that's* tragic.

LEE. Way I see it, for local news to make *any* sense, you've got to have at least a *chance* of shagging the weather girl.

GINGER. Where were we. Oh yes. A ninety-foot giant.

DAVEY. You ask me, *Points West* missed the cunt.

LEE. They was off in Norwich opening a fête.

DAVEY. They was too busy merging with BBC Belgium.

LEE. I believe Johnny. I think they missed him.

PEA. Me too.

DAVEY. A ninety-foot giant. The dozy cunts.

LEE. And that, in a nutshell, is what's wrong with this country.

GINGER *looks at* JOHNNY.

JOHNNY. I never said nothing.

GINGER. Where is it?

JOHNNY. Where's what?

GINGER. Where's the drum?

JOHNNY. What?

GINGER. Where's this giant's drum? His earring. Where's that then?

JOHNNY. You're sitting on it.

GINGER *leaps up. There it is.*

PEA. Fuckin' hell. Look.

TANYA. Fuckin' hell.

LEE. Check it out. It's carved with some weird shit. Runes.

GINGER. Bollocks.

LEE. Go on. Give it a bang.

JOHNNY. I wouldn't do that if I were you. Not unless you mean it. Not unless you really mean it. You don't want to send the signal to all the ancient giants of these isles and when they get here from the four corners have to tell them it's a wrong number.

GINGER. I have literally never heard such bollocks in my life.

JOHNNY. You don't believe me, Ginger.

JOHNNY *gets up, he puts the drum in the middle of the clearing.*

Be my guest.

They all look at the drum.

Something wrong, Ginger?

GINGER. Nothing's fucking wrong. Just... What if I don't feel like it?

JOHNNY. You don't believe me. Go ahead.

GINGER. What, now I have to do everything you say?

JOHNNY. Anyone else want to give it a try?

They all sit there. Suddenly LEE *stands.*

TANYA. Go on, Lee. Go on, my son.

LEE. All right.

He goes over to the drum.

JOHNNY. You feeling brave, Colonel? Give it a go.

LEE *rattles his fingers across it.*

Harder. You want them to hear it, now, don't you?

LEE *bounces his hand off it.*

That's it. Harder. Harder.

LEE *bangs it with his palms. A low roll. Suddenly he stops. Everyone stops.*

LEE. Johnny.

JOHNNY. Come on.

GINGER. Rooster, mate.

JOHNNY *turns.* JOHNNY*'s six-year-old son,* MARKY, *is stood there. Pause.*

JOHNNY. It's all right. Look. Give us a minute.

LEE. All right, you sorry lot. On your feet. At ease. I mean, attention. Let's take a break. Stretch our legs…

JOHNNY. Come back.

LEE. We'll come back, mate.

DAVEY. Yeah, we'll be back. You ain't paid us yet.

GINGER. Come on, Professor.

PROFESSOR. Yes. Yes, of course. A stroll always clears the head, I find.

GINGER. Here we go, mate. Scream if you want to go faster.

Exit all. Pause.

JOHNNY. Don't just bloody stand there. Ain't you got a kiss for me?

MARKY *stands there.*

Come on. Leave me sat here like a pillock.

MARKY *walks over.*

That's better. You got a kiss for me?

MARKY *doesn't want to.*

Come on. Quick smacker. No? Suit yourself.

Enter DAWN. *She looks around.*

Where'd you get those plimsolls? They are very flash. Very, very flash. Very smart. Very smart indeed. Look at you, Marky. Big lad. Bloody hair on your chest next. You want something to drink? Coke. Pepsi? All right, Dawn. Looking well. Everyone's looking them's best.

DAWN (*nods to the banner*). What's that?

JOHNNY. What? (*Looks.*) Oh, that. That's art. I'm entering it for the Turner Prize. Marky? You want some Coke? Pepsi?

DAWN. I got someone waiting for me. Out on the road.

JOHNNY. Right.

DAWN. So we're still on?

JOHNNY. Oh. Right. Yeah. Yes.

DAWN. Good. Don't let him go on the ghost train. He had nightmares for months after last year… I'll come pick him up around five.

JOHNNY. Right. Actually, Dawn. There's a problem. I can't take the boy up the fair today. See, something's come up. It's nothing serious, but it's changed the plan. I can't help it. It's unforeseen.

DAWN. Unforeseen.

WESLEY *comes out of the house, with white powder all over his top lip.*

WESLEY. Crikey. Call that whizz? Tastes like urinal cake. (*Stops.*) Hello, Dawn.

DAWN. Wesley.

WESLEY. Hello, Marky… Uh… Gosh, you're getting big, aren't you, Marky?

JOHNNY. You remember your Uncle Wesley, Marky.

WESLEY. How old are you now? How old are you?

MARKY. Six.

WESLEY. Six years old. Well, well, well.

JOHNNY. He'll be serving you in his pub soon.

WESLEY. Leave it. So. Dawn. How's things over Devizes? You bought a new flat, I hear. Congratulations. Please excuse my appearance, doing some promotion work today. For the pub. I'm the Barley Sword Bearer. (*Pause.*) Yeah. I better be off. Shall I, uh. Pay you now or later. (*Beat.*) I'll pay you later. Nice to see you. Catch you later, Johnny.

JOHNNY. Don't forget your hat.

WESLEY. See ya, Dawn. See ya, Marky. Happy Fair Day.

Exit WESLEY.

DAWN. Go and play indoors.

JOHNNY. Yeah, go and play on the video. I got that Lara Croft. Do a best out of five. Mind the step. And don't open any drawers or cupboards. And don't go in the back room. The floor's up. Mind how you go.

MARKY *heads inside.*

Excuse the mess. We're just giving Lee Piper a send-off. He's off to Australia tomorrow. You know Lee. Good lad. He ain't never even been abroad before, so we're just sending him on his way.

DAWN. What the hell are you doing, John?

JOHNNY. What?

DAWN. 'What?'

JOHNNY. What?

DAWN. Okay. Sure. We can do this. 'What?' I'll tell you what.

Beat.

JOHNNY. Oh, that.

DAWN. 'Oh, that.' Yes, John. 'That.' You know how I know? Marky told me. His mate Dashiell told him. At school. Dashiell's dad's in the South Wiltshire, and he's at a barbecue Sunday, laughing about it with a bunch of the other dads. Everyone at the school gate knows. All the other mums. All the kids. But I call you yesterday, three in the afternoon, you're in the pub. 'Sure, no problem, tomorrow's fine. I'll take Marky up the fair.'

JOHNNY. Dawn –

DAWN. I get here and you're sitting around, getting pissed with a bunch of kids. The police are coming. They're going to bulldoze this place. You're having a party.

JOHNNY. It's a storm in a teacup.

DAWN. Of course. Of course it is. Marky comes home every day in floods. Scratches. Bruises. His bag-handle torn. 'Your dad don't pay no tax. Your dad's a gyppo. He's going to prison.' 'Not my dad, Mum. My dad's great. My dad's the best.' 'He is, Marky. He's amazing. He's a one-off. He can't even take his own boy up the fair. Can't keep a promise to a six-year-old child.' Question: Do you have drugs in there? Where your son is.

JOHNNY. Dawn –

DAWN. Because when the police get here, tomorrow morning, what are they going to find? Because Marky needs that next. You in prison for ten fucking years. Marky needs that like a bag on his head.

JOHNNY. Marky ain't got nothing to worry about. That boy's gonna be just fine.

DAWN. Really. That's a relief. Because, this time Monday, at school. After the South Wiltshire have turned you inside out. Fucking bulldozed this to the ground and you're sat in some cell. Then, Marky's got nothing to worry about. Do you have drugs in there, John?

JOHNNY. Dawn –

DAWN. Do you –

JOHNNY. Dawn –

DAWN. Answer me. Do you have drugs in there –

JOHNNY. You know I fucking do. Why? You want some?

DAWN. Fuck off.

JOHNNY. Dawn –

DAWN. Fuck off. All right? Fuck off. Like I'm in the wrong here. Like this is my fault. My problem. Fuck off.

JOHNNY. Look, Dawn, relax. Sit down, have a drink. It's nothing to worry about.

DAWN. Good. Excellent. Well, let's have a drink then. It's Fair Day. (*Beat.*) What happened, Johnny? The world turns. And it turns. And it moves on and you don't. You're still here.

JOHNNY. You know what they say, Dawn. If it ain't broke.

DAWN. It is broke. It's broke. Like a stopped fucking clock. (*Shows him her watch.*) Wake up. Because when it gets to there – look at it. Look at it – when it gets to there, Johnny –

JOHNNY. You leave all of that to me.

DAWN. I need to use your phone.

JOHNNY. Why?

DAWN. I need to call someone.

JOHNNY. What about the mobile I got you?

DAWN. It got cut off.

JOHNNY. Oh.

DAWN. You buy me a phone for a birthday present – 'Don't worry, Dawn, I'll pay-as-you-go.' Two weeks later, it's dead. It's cut off…

They stare at each other. He fishes out his mobile.

JOHNNY. What's the number?

She won't tell him.

He' ya.

He gives her his phone. JOHNNY *goes over to her bag. He knocks it off the table. Stuff spills out, he looks around in it. Some knitting has spilled out.*

DAWN (*into phone*). Hello. Are you still there? I'm at his place. Look, he's let me down. I know. I know. Look, do you mind if we take Marky to the fair? We can go to Salisbury another day. You're a sweetheart. All right. I'll see you in ten minutes. All right, babe. Ta-da…

She hangs up. Presses more buttons.

JOHNNY. What are you doing?

DAWN. Deleting the number.

Pause.

JOHNNY. So, tell me. How have you been?

DAWN. Me? Terrific. I've met a fantastic man. He gets on great with your boy. How are you?

Beat.

JOHNNY. I mustn't grumble. Though last week was a bad week.

He reaches into his pocket and finds a wrap. He puts the coke onto the top of a Trivial Pursuit box. He takes one of the question cards and starts chopping out lines.

I had a run-in with four Nigerians in Marlborough town centre. Four traffic wardens. See, I'd spent all day in The Bear, and I was walking home when I got caught short. So I pop down a side street and I'm having a Jimmy Riddle on the near back wheel of a people carrier. Suddenly, these four big Nigerians get out. Traffic wardens. They're being picked up and taken back to base. They start shouting. Saying I pissed on their car. Needless to say, I flat deny it. They all crowd round. They say something. I say something. Upshot was, they bundled me in the back and all sat on me. Drove me to this flat on the outskirts of town. I was held captive for a week.

DAWN. You were kidnapped by traffic wardens.

JOHNNY. They tied me up in the basement. That week, I learned more about the life of a Wiltshire traffic warden than I ever thought I'd know. They walk miles. Long days. It's hard, hard graft, for rubbish pay. On day three they brought a TV down and we all watched the snooker semi-final. They said they'd let me go if I said I was sorry. Only problem was, I wasn't. In the end I escaped. See, all week they were bringing me Nigerian delicacies which I chewed up and stored in my pouches. I didn't swallow nothing for a week, and I got thinner and thinner, until the ropes loosened. When they weren't looking, I threw my coat on the fire to muffle the flame, inched up the chimney, out onto the rooftops. I was away. So, that was a rough few days. Apart from that, mustn't grumble.

DAWN *comes over. Does a couple of lines. Walks away. He reaches into her bag on the table again.*

Hello. What's this?

He picks up the knitting.

Booties. Wow-wee. Are you up the pole? Are you pregnant, Dawn? You pregnant again. Bloody hell. You are, aren't you.

DAWN. It's none of your business.

JOHNNY. You having a baby, Dawn?

DAWN. No, I'm not having a baby.

JOHNNY. Then what you knitting booties for? Dawn? What you knitting booties for if you're not having a baby?

DAWN. It's work.

JOHNNY. What?

DAWN. Work. Lots of people do it. It's when you do something and someone pays you for it. (*Beat.*) It's a mail-order company. People with babies what can't knit phone in, or whatever, they ask for hats, jumpers. This woman who owns the company, she has a pool of knitters. I'm one of the knitters.

Beat.

JOHNNY. So what's his name?

He moves to her. Smiles.

Come on. Tom? Pete. Lee. John. Leonard. Quentin. Archibald. Hilary. Wolfgang. Adolf. Beauregard. Cornelius –

DAWN. It's Andy.

JOHNNY. Andy. What kind of stupid name is that?

He touches her hair.

DAWN. Get off me. It's too hot.

JOHNNY. Is it? Too hot, is it?

He kisses her. They kiss. She pulls away.

Pause.

DAWN. Who's looking after you, John?

JOHNNY. Don't you worry about me, darling. I got loads of onlookers. I don't get a moment's peace.

DAWN. Right. Drunk teenagers. You think they give a fuck about you? If they came up here and found you dead in that chair. When you're gone, they'll all say, 'Oh yeah, old what's-his-name. He was a great bloke.' You're on your own. You and the trees. What am I going to tell him? When you're gone?

JOHNNY. Who says I'm going anywhere?

DAWN. Just make sure there's nothing in there when the police get here. Just do that for your son. Me, I don't care. I don't want him growing up on the bus to and from prison.

JOHNNY. What makes you think the South Wiltshire are getting in here? Who says the South Wiltshire are getting within a hundred yards of this place?

DAWN. Right. Of course. I didn't think of that. That's stupid of me. I forgot you're Spiderman. Fucking Supertramp. What planet are you on?

JOHNNY. Same one as you, Dawn. Same one as you. (*Beat.*) Come here.

DAWN. No.

JOHNNY. Come over here. Come over here. I'm not going to try nothing. Just come here, I want to show you something.

DAWN. John –

JOHNNY. I'm serious. Come over here. Come and stand here.

She does.

Good. Now. Look in my eyes. (*Beat.*) Dawn. Look in my eyes. Look at me.

She does.

What do you see?

DAWN. Black.

JOHNNY. Keep looking. Look in my eyes. Deeper. Now I'm going to show you something. Are you ready?

She is. Silence.

Did you see that? Did you see it? (*Pause.*) Did you see it, Dawn?

Pause. She starts to shake.

DAWN. Yes.

Pause.

JOHNNY. Well, now. There now. What's to worry?

MARKY comes out. DAWN looks away, trembling. JOHNNY watches her.

Who won Lara Croft?

MARKY. The telly's gone.

JOHNNY. Oh, right. Yeah. It's gone to the repair shop.

DAWN. Shall we go up the fair, Marky? See your friends. The floats. Go on the rides?

MARKY. Okay.

JOHNNY. Here you go.

He gives MARKY a tenner.

Get some candyfloss, or, like… football cards. I don't know. Have a go on the whirler-swirler. (*To* DAWN.) You gonna come back later? Get rid of what's-his-name, pop back. I'll be here. Come back later. We'll have a drink.

DAWN (*flatly*). Say goodbye to your father, Marky.

MARKY. Goodbye.

JOHNNY. See you later, Marky. You gonna give me a hug before you go? No? Suit yourself. (*To* DAWN.) What about you, Dawn? Before you go?

Pause.

DAWN. Goodbye, Johnny.

Exit DAWN and MARKY. JOHNNY's on his own. He smiles. He stops smiling. He eyes the wood nervously. He goes inside the trailer.

Sounds of applause drift over from the fair.

LEE *and* TANYA *enter.*

TANYA. So, what's in Australia you can't get here?

LEE. Don't know really. Sun. Sand. Surfing. Adventure. Excitement. The unknown. Thrill of discovery. Spiritual growth. Perspective. New horizons. Here. Did you know there are ley lines running through this wood?

TANYA. Ley what?

LEE. Ley lines. There's a ley line runs clean through this wood. Clean through this copse.

TANYA. Fuck's a ley line?

LEE. Ley lines is lines of ancient energy, stretching across the landscape. Linking ancient sites. Like this one, the one you've got here goes… (*Thinks.*) Avebury Standing Stones, through Silbury Hill, right down to Stonehenge, and on to Glastonbury. That ley line comes clean through here. We're standing on it right now. Seriously. If you was a Druid, this wood is holy. This is holy land.

TANYA. Okay. I just want to be absolutely sure we're on the same page. When I say free, I mean no strings. Even if I get pregnant.

LEE. It's not that I don't appreciate it, Tanya.

TANYA. Bollocks, Piper. If you're not going to eat my peaches, don't shake my tree.

LEE. Tanya, I've listened to the offer. I respect the offer. I do not want to eat your peaches.

Beat.

TANYA. Your move, bender.

They look at each other. Beat.

PEA *and the* PROFESSOR *come back.*

PEA. Here we go, Professor. How's that?

PROFESSOR. Much better, thank you, Pea. Much better.

PEA. You sit down there.

TANYA (*indicating the lines of coke*). Pea.

> PEA *and* TANYA *start doing the lines of coke on the Trivial Pursuit box.*

> GINGER *enters with* DAVEY.

DAVEY. What you doing?

PEA. What, nothing.

LEE. What is it?

TANYA. Coke, mate.

DAVEY. Lush.

LEE. Sweet.

TANYA. Sorry, mate. Snooze, you lose.

DAVEY. Bastards. Let me lick the board. Let me lick the card.

> PEA *licks the card and gives him the finger.*

> After all the controlled substances I've given you down the years. That's the thanks I get.

PEA (*reading the card*). For ten points. What was found under the patio of 10 Brookside Close?

DAVEY. Fuck off.

GINGER. Pass.

PEA. Lee.

LEE. I can't believe you just did that.

DAVEY. How many lines were there?

PEA. Professor?

PROFESSOR. I'm afraid I can't help.

PEA. Tanya.

TANYA. No idea.

PEA. Anyone?

JOHNNY (*from inside*). Bzzz. Trevor Jordache's body.

    Beat. PEA *and* TANYA *laugh.*

PEA. Is correct. Who was the star of *Paper Tiger*?

TANYA. Paper who?

DAVEY. No idea.

JOHNNY. Bzz. David Niven.

PEA. Question three. How many English horse races are defined as 'Classics'?

JOHNNY. Bzzz. Five. 2,000 Guineas, 1,000 Guineas, Oaks, Derby and St Leger.

TANYA. How the fuck does he know that?

    JOHNNY *bursts out.*

JOHNNY. All right. You want to play a game? Make some money. You lot against me. First to twenty. If you win, I'll give you all fifty quid.

DAVEY. Bollocks.

JOHNNY. A hundred. A hundred quid each to anyone who beats me.

    He gets out a roll of money. Slaps it on the table.

DAVEY. Deal.

PEA. Rooster.

LEE. Are you sure?

JOHNNY. Two hundred Australian, Lee. Two hundred Australian. I'll tell you what. That's a grand. All of that is yours if you win.

PEA. Fuck me.

TANYA. Jesus!

DAVEY. Come on, boy!

JOHNNY. All of you against me.

ALL. Come on, then.

PEA. Okay. Here go. Which word indicates that a liquid is able to resist flowing?

JOHNNY. Bzzz. Viscous. Or viscosity.

PEA. Which is the largest body of water to come under the auspices of Bolivia's six-thousand-man army?

JOHNNY. Bzzz. Lake Titicaca. What?

DAVEY. How the fuck do you know that?

JOHNNY. Everyone knows that. You've got a buzzer. Use it. You know the answer, use it.

PEA. Which composer was the first to win three Oscars for –

JOHNNY. Bzzz. Marvin Hamlisch.

GINGER. What's going on?

JOHNNY. What? You've got a buzzer. Use it.

PEA. Which play includes the line: 'Blest are those whose blood and judgement – '

JOHNNY. Bzzz. *Hamlet.*

GINGER. You have learned these sodding questions.

JOHNNY. What are you talking about? Are you accusing me of cheating? Just say yes or no. Are you accusing me of cheating?

GINGER. Yes.

JOHNNY. If you are, get out of my wood.

PEA. What does a praying mantis have one of that most men have two of?

JOHNNY. Bzzz. Ears. One ear.

TANYA. No.

DAVEY. How do you know that then?

JOHNNY. Like I've got time to sit around learning every question… Who d'you think I am?

GINGER. I know what you're doing, Byron, you cunt.

JOHNNY. Look. How sad would I have to be to sit and learn every question of every card of the fucking Genus 2000 Edition of Trivial Pursuit? If you're saying I'm that sad, get off my land.

GINGER. I ain't playing.

JOHNNY. You lot are a bunch of losers. If you don't know nothing you should've said.

They all start picking up cards, laughing, amazed.

TANYA. Who did Pravda refer to as 'nothing more than a glorified FBI – '

JOHNNY. Bzzz. Superman.

ALL. Fuckin' hell –

   Fuckin' cheat –

   Dirty bastard –

   Cheating Arab –

   I'm not playing –

PEA. What brush-cleaning chemical –

JOHNNY. Bzzz. Turpentine.

TANYA. Which titled detective –

JOHNNY. Bzzz. Lord Peter Wimsey.

PEA. Which archipelago –

JOHNNY. Bzzz. Tierra del Fuego.

DAVEY. Fucking come on, Professor. There's fifty quid on this. We're going down in flames.

They look at the PROFESSOR. *He's absolutely stationary.*

Professor?

PEA. Professor?

LEE. Man down.

GINGER. Look out. Elvis has left the building.

PEA. He's dead.

TANYA. Oh my God!

DAVEY. He's sparko.

GINGER. He ain't dead. Look at him. He's having the time of his life.

JOHNNY. Come on, you losers, come on.

PEA. Which Olympic race –

JOHNNY. Bzzz. 50,000 metre walk.

TANYA. Which two letters –

JOHNNY. Bzzzz. D and E.

TANYA. – did Daniel Defoe add to his name?

GINGER. Congratulations, Johnny. You're the winner.

DAVEY. Who was the first professional cricketer –

JOHNNY. Bzzzzz. Sir Len Hutton.

DAVEY. – to captain England?

PEA. Which –

JOHNNY. Bzzz. Eric Cantona.

DAVEY. When –

JOHNNY. Bzzzz. 1492.

DAVEY. Wrong.

PEA. Which –

JOHNNY. Bzzzz. Pink Floyd.

PEA. Wrong.

LEE. What –

JOHNNY. Bzzzz… The milling on the edge of a one-pound coin.

LEE. Is correct. How the fuck did he do that?

JOHNNY. I'm magic, me. Fuckin' magic Johnny Byron. I got X-ray vision. I'm Spiderman, me. I bet you fifty quid to ten pence I get the next one.

GINGER. Who wrote the words to the popular hymn 'Jerusalem'?

Pause.

JOHNNY. Ah, fuck. I know this. Fuck. It's…

GINGER. Johnny.

JOHNNY. Wait.

LEE. Johnny.

JOHNNY *turns, looks off. A big man,* TROY WHITWORTH, *enters the clearing.*

JOHNNY. Troy. Good afternoon, mate. Welcome to our banquet. Welcome to our Bucolic Alcoholic Frolic. Pull up a chair. Lee.

LEE. What?

JOHNNY. Get up. Let Mr Whitworth sit down. Everyone, I think you know Troy. Troy, I think you know everyone here. How's the fair, mate? You win anything yet?

TROY. You having a party then?

JOHNNY. Big day, ain't it? Pull up a chair, mate. What are you drinking these days?

TROY. I ain't staying.

JOHNNY. It's no bother, Troy. Shift up, girls. Make room.

TROY. I said, I ain't staying.

JOHNNY. Don't be daft. You slog all the way up here. Let's have a drink –

TROY. You deaf, gyppo? I ain't sitting with you.

JOHNNY. You busy today? You on the floats?

TROY. Where is she?

JOHNNY. What?

TROY. Don't try my patience. Where is she? Where's Phaedra?

JOHNNY. Phaedra. (*Beat.*) Hang about. Which one's she?

TROY. Don't try me, Byron.

JOHNNY. What's she look like?

TROY. Do not try me. You know who she is.

JOHNNY. I can't tell these rats apart, Troy. Not one from the other. I wouldn't worry yourself, mate. She'll be back. (*Beat.*) Wait. Phaedra. I got her. Small. Brown hair. Freckles. Big eyes? I tell you, boy. She's a sweetheart. Lovely big eyes. She's a treasure, though. Ain't she the May Queen? Queen of the Fair? If she is then she gotta be back. She don't want to miss that, then, do she? I remember when she won last year. Pretty dress. Her hair all… Shaking like a leaf, she was, when they told her. When they put on the crown. I remember how she wept. Best day of her life, she said, to the Mayor. I wouldn't worry, mate. She'll be back. She's not gonna wanna miss a day like that.

Pause.

TROY. Get rid of them.

JOHNNY. Look, Troy –

TROY. Tell them to fuck off. This is between you and me.

JOHNNY. Look. There's no need to break up the party.
Thought we were mates, Troy. Your brothers, Frank and
Danny, last summer they was always up here. Playing
Swingball. Cards. They're good lads. I don't have no beef
with the Whitworths.

TROY. Get rid of them. Now.

JOHNNY. Troy, mate. What say we bury the hatchet?

TROY. You deaf as well as daft? We'll bury the hatchet all
right. Right in your fuckin' skull, pikey. You *did*. You
diddicoy maggot. Living on a rubbish tip. Worzel Maggot.
Stig of the Dump. Thinks he's the Pied Piper. You're the
lowest piece of shit in this forest, mate. It's you and me now,
you fucking snake. I will beat you into your grave. Into your
grave, Gypsy. Now, one more time, cunt. Where's my
daughter?

PEA. She ain't your daughter.

TROY. Shut it, slapper.

JOHNNY. Troy –

PEA. Don't call me a slapper.

TROY. Just fucking open your cockhole one more time, I'll shut
it for good. Shut the fuck up. You wanna say some more?
Little bitch. Little cocksucker.

GINGER. Hang on.

TROY. You want some, you lanky cunt?

GINGER. No.

TROY. Then shut your greasy cakehole, maggot. I ain't talking
to you.

GINGER. Sorry.

Pause.

JOHNNY. Mate. You're worried. Christ, what father wouldn't
be? She's young. Fifteen. She shouldn't be stopping out. It's

not right. Not safe. I understand, mate. You're just worried. It's not just you feel a little bit randy today.

Pause.

TROY. What did you say?

Pause.

JOHNNY. You miss her, boy? She your treasure? I remember you in the pub, last Fair Night, buying drinks. Toasting her name. 'I got the Queen of Flintock under my roof.' Bet it's hard to sleep with her right next door. She in your dreams, boy? She in your dreams?

TROY. Shut your fucking mouth.

JOHNNY. Put me wrong if you're made right, boy. If you're made right. I'm standing here. Put me wrong.

TROY. I'll mark you good, gyppo. I'll put you in the ground.

Pause.

JOHNNY. When was it you were last up here, Troy. Last in this wood? Jesus, I don't think I've seen you up here since you were fifteen, sixteen years old. Shooting cans. Smoking. You and those other two, rain or shine. Do you remember that night we took a pack of cards? The old ones with the devils on the back. And we laid them in a circle. Just in there, in the dead of night. It was pitch dark. We poured a glass of wine into a plate, a silver plate, like a blood-red mirror, and you took the candle and you gazed into the mirror. (*Beat.*) You shook like a leaf. You couldn't stop shaking. Couldn't speak. You were terrified, boy. From that day, you stopped coming to see me. From that day, you never came back. Have you come to play again, boy? I still got the cards. You want to play again?

TROY *looks at him for some time. He starts to laugh.*

TROY. Ain't changed much, has it. Except the faces. All except Ginger here. He was here when I was here. What happened, mate? Got lost? Can't find your way home?

(*Laughs.*) I tell you, Rooster, Frank and Danny was up here all last summer and they'd come home four, five in the morning, tell me all the stories. All the tales. Took me back, it done. 'Nothing changes up there,' I says. They told me this one. End of June, it was. They're coming through here, seven in the evening, go see the Rooster, shake him awake. Get the fire going. Have a gasp. They're coming over, guess what they find? Lying out, on the path. Down in the dirt, smashed out his mind. Sparko. Bottle of own-brand, out fucking cold. Couldn't even make it home. You'd pissed yourself. Pissed all over your trousers, your coat. And, you know what they done? They undone their flies and they pissed on you too. All overs you. On your face. In your hair. In your mouth. Took photos with their phones. Sent it to everyone. I bet Lee there's got it on his phone. Pea. Tanya. I know Davey has. He filmed it. Show him, Davey. Show Rooster what you done. They told me all the stories, Rooster. Took me right back. Nothing changes up here.

Pause.

When you're alone, gyppo. When you're alone.

Pause. The others look ashamed. Exit TROY. *Silence.*

GINGER. When we was in school, he had the worst eczema I have ever seen. Used to call him Cornflakes. He was always a wanker, too.

Silence.

LEE. Ginger –

Pause. They stand there. Eventually, JOHNNY *turns, and walks off. Silence.*

Thanks.

DAVEY. What? What did I do?

Silence.

LEE. Fucking great.

DAVEY. I just filmed it, mate. I never done nothing. You had it on your phone for ages.

Silence.

PEA. I can't believe you done that.

DAVEY. Fuck off. You laughed at it all right.

PEA. Yeah, but it's not funny, is it. It's not funny.

GINGER. Great.

PEA. What?

GINGER. That is great. I'm coming up.

DAVEY. Oh, I forgot about that.

LEE. Marvellous.

GINGER. I'm tripping. Now I'm going to have a nightmare one. Fantastic. Great.

LEE. Look, we better go.

DAVEY. I ain't been paid yet.

LEE. Shut up, will you. Come on.

DAVEY. What did I say?

PEA. What about him?

GINGER. We'll come back for him. I'll come back. I'll iron this all out.

PEA. Let's get out of here.

GINGER. I'll come back. I'll iron this out.

Exit GINGER, LEE, PEA *and* DAVEY. *Apart from the* PROFESSOR, *the clearing is empty. We hear the Tannoy drift over from the fair.*

Silence.

PROFESSOR. There was a knight born in Cappadocia. (*Pause.*) On a time he came in to the province of Libya, to a city named Silene. And by this city was a stagnant pond wherein dwelled a dragon which envenomed all the country. And when he came nigh the city he scorched the people with his breath. There was an ordinance made in the town that there should be taken the children and young people of the town by lot, and every each one as it fell, were he gentle or poor, should be delivered unto the beast. Now, in time a noble knight passed, and when he beheld the mighty creature, said unto the citizens: 'Now doubt ye no thing, without more, believe ye in God, Jesu Christ, and do ye to be baptised and I shall slay the dragon!'

The trailer door opens. PHAEDRA, *still dressed as a fairy, comes out. She approaches the edge of the clearing and looks out. Shaking. Trembling. Shallow breathing. Suddenly it stops. She holds her breath and we...*

Blackout.

End of Act Two.

ACT THREE

Five o'clock. A Spitfire flies over. A distant crowd cheer. The church bell sounds.

Enter DAVEY *and* LEE. *Both in sunglasses.* LEE *has his 'FARE WELL LEE?' T-shirt on, and a goldfish in a bag.* DAVEY *is holding a giant toy rabbit, cuddly, practically the size of him. They each have candyfloss.* DAVEY *and* LEE *lift up their sunglasses and look around.*

LEE *knocks on the door.*

LEE. Rooster. It's us. Open up. (*Knocks.*) Rooster? Rooster. Open the door. (*He bangs on the door.*) Johnny, mate. It's Lee and Davey. We've come… we've come to say sorry.

DAVEY. No we ain't.

LEE. Shut up. Yes we have.

DAVEY. No we ain't. We've come for whizz.

LEE. Shut up, will you.

DAVEY. I've come for whizz.

LEE. Rooster! (*Knocks.*) Rooster, mate?

Enter GINGER, *in a pith helmet and shades, holding a coconut.*

DAVEY. You all right, Corporal?

GINGER. Visual, mate. Very visual. Basically brilliant in the legs. Good in the middle. The top third's iffy. Blinding headache. Basically, it feels like I've got, like, this incredibly heavy hundred-pound weight on my head.

LEE. Permission to take hat off.

GINGER. What? What hat?

LEE. The one on your head, mate. The one you won on the bric-a-brac.

GINGER. What are you talking about? (*Looks up.*) Oh, that. That won't come off.

LEE. Try.

GINGER. I've tried. I can't get it off.

LEE. You want a hand?

GINGER. No, don't fucking touch it.

LEE. Mate. Give me the coconut.

GINGER. Don't take my coconut.

LEE. Ginge –

GINGER. I'm serious. Do *not* touch my coconut.

LEE. You're just high. Put the coconut down.

GINGER. Fuck off. Don't make me use this.

LEE. Drop it. Drop the coconut…

GINGER. Do – Not – Make – Me – Use – This.

LEE. Okay. Just put it down. On the floor. One. Two. Three.

GINGER *puts the coconut on the floor.*

And rest. How was that?

GINGER. I don't want to talk about it.

LEE. All right. Do this. All right. Copy me. Ready. One. Two. Three.

LEE *mimes taking a hat off.* GINGER *lifts the pith helmet off.*

GINGER. Oh God. That's better. That's so much better. That was like a vice. That was awful. It was like my ears couldn't breathe.

LEE. You're all right now, mate. Settle. Regroup.

GINGER. I'm back on top. That is so much better. I was momentarily in trouble there. (*To* LEE.) Is he there?

LEE. I don't know. (*Knocks.*)

DAVEY. Here, Ginger. I just got a texter from 2 Trevs and one Trev said he'd had a punch-up with the other Trev, and they've split up.

GINGER (*stops*). What?

DAVEY. They've disbanded. 2 Trevs is no more. They've gone home. You want to get up The Cooper's car park. Your public awaits.

GINGER. But... I'm... I'm... I'm... I'm... I'm... I'm... I'm... I'm... I'm... I'm...

DAVEY. It's your big break, mate.

GINGER. I'm roasted.

DAVEY. Use it, mate. Boss the stone, mate. Get up on top and boss it. Your canvas is The Cooper's car park, your brush Beyoncé and 'The Birdie Song'. It is time to bring the ruckus.

GINGER. I don't have my decks. My records.

DAVEY. Then go get your records. Get a move on. Time waits for no man. *Carpe diem.*

GINGER. Hang on. Hang on. Hang about. This is bullshit.

DAVEY. Can you be sure of that?

GINGER *considers this.*

GINGER. Fuck me. I need a sit-down.

DAVEY. You've not got time, mate. You're on in a hour.

GINGER *goes and sits down. Stands up. Picks up his coconut.*

GINGER. I'm just going to go for a short walk. I gotta walk this off. Hold that thought.

He wanders off.

DAVEY (*calling after him*). Here, mate. Flintock's this way. Come back! (*Laughs.*) I tell you. I am. I am such a cunt.

LEE (*knocks*). Rooster, mate. It's Lee. I just want to say goodbye, mate.

DAVEY. You ask me. The day they built the New Estate, Rooster's drinking in the last-chance saloon. You watch. A year from now there'll be fifty new houses right here. The New Estate will be the Old Estate, and shit will still be brown. Because that – (*He pulls out his shirt to make tits and emits an impressive alto warble.*) – that is the fat lady singing.

LEE *knocks again. Hangs his goldfish on a hook on the porch.*

What you doing?

LEE. It's a present.

DAVEY. I wouldn't worry too much, boy. Rooster Byron's got a heart of stone. (*Off* LEE*'s look.*) What did I do? Mate. Number one, I never pissed on him. I just filmed it. Don't shoot the messenger.

LEE. It's not funny.

DAVEY. It was when I showed you it.

LEE. Well, it ain't funny now.

DAVEY. I suppose you had to be there. (*Beat.*) You ready for your dreamquest then? Ready to go? Only a few hours left, mate.

LEE *looks at his watch. Puts his head in his hands.*

LEE. I was supposed to have a quiet one.

DAVEY. 6 a.m. You miss that bus, you're stuck in Flintock for ever. You want another tab?

LEE. Fuck off. (*To himself.*) I gotta sober up.

DAVEY. Why do you want to change your name?

LEE. I don't want to change my name.

DAVEY. Seriously, why do you –

LEE. You wouldn't understand.

DAVEY. Try me, Lee Piper. Try me.

LEE. You're David Dean.

DAVEY. Yes, mate.

LEE. David Dean from Flintock.

DAVEY. Absolutely.

LEE. Nothing else.

DAVEY. Nothing but.

LEE. Never nothing else? Just David Dean.

DAVEY. Not ever. Not once. (*Pause.*) My name's David Dean. I
    work in the abattoir. Get there six in the morning – hungover,
    hazmat suit, goggles – and I stand there and I slay two
    hundred cows. Wham. Next contestant. What's your name
    and where d'you come from? (*Mimes killing a cow.*) Wham!
    Have lunch. Pot Noodle. Come back. Slay two hundred
    more. End of the week, I walk out of there. I'll tell you what
    I ain't thinking. I ain't thinking: 'Perhaps I'll change my
    name. Get a Celtic tattoo. See this on my arse? That
    symbolises the Harmony of the Spheres. That's Vishnu, God
    of Gayness.' I'll tell you what I'm thinking: 'Shag on. It's the
    weekend. Pay me. Show me the paper, and shag on.' I wish
    you well on your quest, Frodo. But whatever you change
    your name to, you're still fucking Lee Piper; and wherever
    you go in this world, when you get off the plane, boat, train
    or crawl out of the jungle smeared in paint, the bloke waiting
    to meet you is also called Lee Piper. Make paper. Make more
    paper. Shag on.

LEE. That's why you're always broke.

DAVEY. What?

LEE. Ever since I've known you. Come Tuesday, you ain't never got a pound for a saveloy. You're broke.

DAVEY. What's your point, Lee Piper?

LEE. Seriously, though, I'm not being funny, but you… You, mate. You are a sad, fat povvo what thinks he's Alan Sugar. You're going to live your whole life with the same fucking people, going to the same shit pubs, kill two million cows, and die a sad, fat povvo.

DAVEY. Sounds unimprovable.

LEE *laughs.* DAVEY *throws his arms wide.* LEE *shakes his head.*

Seriously. Where do you want me to sign?

LEE *laughs. Pause.*

LEE. I don't want to go.

DAVEY. Yes you do.

LEE. I don't.

DAVEY. You do.

LEE. I fucking don't.

DAVEY. Tough. You're going. Yes you are.

LEE. Bollocks. You can't make me.

DAVEY. I fucking can.

LEE. No you can't.

DAVEY. If I have to carry you. If I have to carry you to Chippenham. If I have to carry you to Australia. Because that's where you're going. That's where you're going, 6 a.m. tomorrow.

Beat.

LEE. David Dean.

DAVEY (*sniffs*). Stop. Smell that. Smell the air.

LEE. What am I smelling?

DAVEY. That. Smell it.

Beat.

BOTH. What is that?

LEE. That's beautiful.

DAVEY. Right there. That's it.

LEE. That's what I'm talking about.

DAVEY. Just breathe that in. That's it. Right there. One last
time.

LEE. That's it, mate. That's it.

DAVEY (*singing*).
      With the merry ring, adieu the merry spring –

BOTH (*singing*).
      For summer is a-come unto day,
      How happy is the little bird that merrily doth sing,
      In the merry morning of May.

      Unite and unite,
      For summer is a-come unto day,
      And wither we are going, we all unite,
      In the merry morning of May!

They leave, 'singing'. JOHNNY *appears from the trees,
watches them walk away. Another Spitfire flies over.*

WESLEY (*offstage*). Byron, you cunt.

Enter WESLEY. *He's drunk.*

JOHNNY. Wesley.

WESLEY. There you are, you old cunt. There you are, you
shitter.

JOHNNY. So where are we?

WESLEY. The Mayor is in the stocks outside The Moonrakers, and kids are chucking sponges at him. There was a punch-up in the slots. Ian Brindle pushed over the mobile toilet with Danny Anstey inside it. Marlborough won the tug-of-war.

JOHNNY. You look hot, Wesley. You been dancing?

WESLEY. Dancing? I been dancing all day, lover. Like a dancing chimpanzee. Fuckin' danced halfway from here to Land's End. Don't talk to me about fucking dancing.

JOHNNY. Pub full then?

WESLEY. Fall of Saigon, mate. Sue's got three extra staff on. I went behind the bar, she told me 'hop it'. Said I were, quote, 'ostensibly pissed'. Some bloke from the brewery's there. About twenty bloody years old. Like the fucking KGB, that lot. (*Beat.*) Public bar, saloon bar, pool table, *Millionaire* machine, shit burgers, crap kiddies' option, fiddly bloody sachets, broken bloody towel dispensers, fucking stupid T-shirts… (*Pause.*) I come to bed when the last cunt's gone home. I lie there next to her and I can't breathe. 'Did you cash up. Lock up? Wash out the trays? Well done, love. Sleep well, my darling.' How much does that cost, eh? I'm the reason that pub's full five nights a week. Swindon knows that. Last Monday, lunchtime, the regional lays five brochures on the bar. Take your pick. The Plume in Devizes, The Mason's in Salisbury, The Green Man in Oxford, somewhere in Banbury. And somewhere else in somewhere else. All good inns. Take your pick. Who do they bring the fucking brochures to? Sue? Bollocks. Me. They trust me. Sometimes I want to take Sue and drive her off into the middle of nowhere… Stupid… bloody… bitch. I never even touched the bloody cash'n'carry card… (*Pause.*) Number one, work all your life. Number two, be nice to people…

He lies down and starts crying.

JOHNNY. I wouldn't lie down too long there, Wesley. Crows'll have your eyes.

WESLEY. Last week, I come downstairs to do the pub quiz questions, bit of peace and quiet, heard Debbie and Pam, barmaids, talking about me. Saying horrible things. Horrible. (*Pause.*) I was in love with Pam for about four years. I've never told anyone that before. (*He cries.*) I can't go back there. Ever, ever, again. I can't.

JOHNNY. Wesley. Go home.

WESLEY. Fuck off.

JOHNNY. Go home, Wesley.

WESLEY. No.

JOHNNY. Take your bells off. Have a shower. Put on a clean shirt, have coffee, get behind the saloon bar, pinch Sue's bum.

WESLEY. No bloody fear.

JOHNNY. Tell her it's from Rooster. Trust me, she loves it.

WELSEY. I wonder where they went. All the Queens of Flintock. I wonder where they are now. (*Beat.*) Heather Bloom. Alice Witherspoon. Margaret Bailey. Wendy Davey. Alexis Wetherley. Jennifer Reynolds. Jennifer Jackson. Angela Delmar. I wonder where they are. I wonder where they are today. (*Pause.*) I'm going for a walk. I'm going up Orr Hill. Watch the trains. You wanna come?

JOHNNY. Another day, mate.

WESLEY. Another day.

Pause. Enter PARSONS *and* FAWCETT.

Right. I better be getting back. I've got a busy night ahead. Anyways, the long and short of it is, you're barred, mate. I don't want you near The Cooper's till further notice. I can't have that nonsense going on. It's a family pub. We have standards. Professional standards. Have I made myself clear?

JOHNNY. Perfectly.

WESLEY. Good. Well, I hope you learn your lesson. You have been warned.

He passes PARSONS *and* FAWCETT.

Afternoon. Afternoon.

Exit WESLEY.

FAWCETT. Mr Byron. Mr John Winston Byron.

JOHNNY. Who wants to know?

FAWCETT. I'm Linda Fawcett, Senior Community Liaison Officer for Kennet and Avon County Council. This is my colleague, Luke Parsons.

PARSONS. Afternoon.

FAWCETT. I see, sir, you found our paperwork. I shall assume it was received and that you've read and digested the contents. Mr Byron, on March 17th you were served with an F-99 enforcement notice. After refusing to reply to or acknowledge receipt of six subsequent summons, this morning you were granted an optional grace period of eight hours to vacate. You now have just over two hours to submit to the enforcement notice and quit this site or you will be forcibly evicted.

Silence. JOHNNY *looks from one to the other.*

JOHNNY. Tell me, Mrs Fawcett. Have we met before?

FAWCETT. Mr Byron, you know full well who I am. We've met many times.

JOHNNY. I knew it. I never forget a face.

FAWCETT. We met in Salisbury Magistrates' Court three years ago when I gave evidence against you in the dispute with my colleagues Pat Pickles.

JOHNNY (*thinks*). Pickles. Pickles…

FAWCETT. You trespassed on Mr Pickles's property, verbally assaulted him, stripped him bare, gagged him and locked him in his shed.

JOHNNY. It's not ringing any bells.

FAWCETT. He was in there without food or water for a week.

JOHNNY. Pickles. Short. Bald. Shifty fat bastard?

FAWCETT. Mr Pickles has high blood pressure, sir. He had no access to his medicine. He lost two and a half stone. He was severely dehydrated. He could have died.

JOHNNY. Pat Pickles should thank me. I called his GP and she said I lowered his blood pressure. She reckoned I've put a good ten years on Pat Pickles.

FAWCETT. Then six months ago you attacked my colleague Peter Hands in the foyer of the Salisbury Arts Centre during the interval of *Jack and the Beanstalk*.

JOHNNY. First of all, that was by far the worst pantomime I've ever been to. I was only there because my mate Tonka helped build the beanstalk. And second, what were you doing at the Christmas pantomime with Mr Hands, a married man who's not your husband?

FAWCETT. For your information, Peter and I won joint first prize in the office sweepstake.

JOHNNY. I see. That's strange, because I was in the row behind you and from where I was sat Mr Hands is aptly named. He's behind you!

She stares at him. PARSONS *lowers the camera.*

PARSONS (*quietly*). I can delete that.

FAWCETT. This illegal encampment has passed unchallenged since September 1982, a period of twenty-seven years, during which time no ground rent or rates have been paid to Kennet and Avon Council.

JOHNNY. Come on, Linda. This is me you're talking to.

FAWCETT. This land belongs to Kennet and Avon Council.

JOHNNY. Says who?

FAWCETT. The law, Mr Byron. The English law. I am showing the recipient a legally recognised petition of local complainants concerning the illegal encampment and activities hereabouts.

JOHNNY. See that sign? What does it say?

FAWCETT. It says, 'Fuck the New Estate', Mr Byron.

JOHNNY. I loves it when you talk dirty, Linda.

FAWCETT. Mr Byron. Your disagreement is not with the New Estate. There are three hundred and twelve residents on the New Estate. There are over two hundred and eighty names recorded here. Would you care to read?

JOHNNY. What are you talking about?

FAWCETT. We went door to door, Mr Byron. Eighty per cent of the population of Flintock have taken time out of their busy days to protest against you.

JOHNNY. Read me those names.

PARSONS (*reads*). Francis Morgan. Donald Morgan.

JOHNNY. Don and Fran Morgan. Don Morgan thinks I did him out of a painting two years back, over in Orr.

PARSONS. Olive Phillips. Jessica Harding. Sydney Harding. Darrell Kerr.

JOHNNY. Darrell still owes me for a lawnmower from nineteen-eighty-bloody-nine.

PARSONS. Percy Lyle. Kate Brindle.

JOHNNY. Percy Lyle runs The Moonrakers, and we've had disagreements for years. It's all cleared up now.

PARSONS. Gordon Baker. Janet Baker. Roland Gosling. Hannah Wilks. Dave Stroyer. Perry Stroyer. Jack Stroyer. Mavis Lennox. Phil Lennox. Bel Tyrell. Lesley Tyrell. Harry Spurling. Meg Spurling.

JOHNNY. Harry and Meg Spurling. They had this dog, right...
and...

Pause.

PARSON. Lee Purvis.

JOHNNY. Never heard of him.

PARSON. Jack Tranter.

JOHNNY. Jack Tranter's a cunt.

PARSONS. Nick Arthur. Paul Austin.

JOHNNY. Never heard of 'em.

PARSONS. Mark Tominey. Mary Tominey. Harry Fields.
Gladys Fields. Jason Kettle. Lily Kettle. Marcus Kettle. Paul
Kettle. Laura Butcher. Gary Forbes. John Metcalfe. Jeremy
Applegate. Lydia Applegate. Danny Anstey. Rebecca Anstey.
Peter Andrews. John Allen. Jennifer Noble. Melanie
Ramsburty. Tom Bloom. Heather Bloom. Kim Angel.

JOHNNY. Okay, stop.

PARSONS. Christopher Angel. Mick Winterslow. Kate Barley.
Jonathan Barley. Tim Barley. Jane Barley. Wendy Coleman.
Walter Coleman.

JOHNNY. I said stop. Enough.

Silence.

Look on the map. This is Rooster's Wood. I'm Rooster
Byron. I'm –

FAWCETT. You are a drug dealer, Mr Byron. You deal drugs
to minors. We have sworn statements. South Wiltshire
police have compiled a dossier of evidence which they will
present in the event of any further resistance. Right now
there's a bulldozer parked on Upavon Road. Tomorrow it
will be joined by two dozen constables. Come 9 a.m.
tomorrow, if you refuse to comply with this order, your
camp will be razed, your vehicles and belongings will be

seized as evidence, you will be arrested. It's over, Byron. We have you.

Silence.

JOHNNY. How many houses are you building? Who gets the contract? Who gets the kickbacks? You're right. Kids come here. Half of them are safer here than they are at home. You got nowhere else to go, come on over. The door's open. You don't like it, stay away. What the fuck do you think an English forest is for?

Pause.

He looks into the camera.

Here ye. This is Rooster Byron, telling all you Kennet and Avon, South Wiltshire bandits and Salisbury white wigs. Bang your gavels. Issue your warrants. You can't make the wind blow. If you want to see your babes again. Your beds. Your electric blankets. Take your leaflets and your meetings and your Borstal and your beatings and your Health and fucking Safety and pack your whole, poxy, sham-faced plot and get. Or there's blood on the chalk before we're through. This is your last and final warning. Hear ye! Hear ye!

FAWCETT. You have till 9 a.m. Good day, Mr Byron.

Exit FAWCETT and PARSONS.

JOHNNY *takes the petition. He sets fire to it. Puts it in a metal container. Watches it burn. He takes out a bottle of Jack Daniel's. He pours it into a pint glass. Drinks it down in one.*

Enter the PROFESSOR, garlanded with flowers. Daisy chains. Flowers for buttons. A crown of blossom. He stops and observes.

PROFESSOR. Is that you, Mr Byron?

JOHNNY. I'll be just a moment. Looks like you've had a good day?

PROFESSOR. What? Oh. Yes. Yes indeed. I've had an
extraordinary day, Mr Byron. I went to a village fair. I had a
pint of beer. Then the next thing I remember is waking alone,
in this wood, on a bed of bracken. All around me were
outstretched green hands, supporting me, surrounding me,
swaying in time with the sunlight. A million tiny green
fingers, the tips scorched by the sun. And amid the bracken,
an army of spiders were building a webbed citadel, with
many bridges and rooms and grand windows and staircases.
All I could hear was birdsong. Crystal clear. It was Mary. I
heard Mary. Calling me. 'Mary! It's you. You've come back
to me. Mary, my dear.' But then I rememebered. That's not
Mary. That can't be Mary… She's gone.

Pause.

JOHNNY. Yes, she is.

PROFESSOR. And she'll never come back.

JOHNNY. No, Professor. I don't believe she will.

Beat.

PROFESSOR. I feel suddenly light. Like I'm in the middle of
light. Like a flame. Or a dancer. I feel light. Like pure light.
(*Beat.*) Well, I better toddle off. The gardener's off on
holiday to Greece. I mustn't forget to pay him before he flies.

JOHNNY. You better.

The PROFESSOR *smiles. He suddenly stops and sniffs the
air.*

PROFESSOR. What is that? What is that scent? I've been
breathing that all day. What can it be?

JOHNNY. That's wild garlic. Wild garlic and the May blossom.

PROFESSOR. Of course. That's what it is. It's been there all
day, and I've only just noticed. Then it's really true. The
winter is over.

(*Singing.*)
> With the merry ring, adieu the merry spring,
> For summer is a-come unto day,
> How happy is the little bird that merrily doth sing,
> In the merry morning of May.

Exit the PROFESSOR. JOHNNY *watches him leave.*
PHAEDRA *comes out of the trailer.*

PHAEDRA. Have they gone? Who are they, Johnny? What do they want?

JOHNNY. They're from the Palace. They've given me a knighthood, for my services to the community.

She shivers. Looks at the goldfish.

PHAEDRA. What's that?

JOHNNY. It just showed up.

PHAEDRA. When? How?

JOHNNY. Search me. I turned round and there it was.

PHAEDRA. What, like a gift?

JOHNNY. Something like that.

PHAEDRA. Who gave it to you?

JOHNNY. A boy passed by. On his way to Chippenham. Left that there.

PHAEDRA. So it's yours.

JOHNNY. I suppose it is.

PHAEDRA. Do you know what to do? How to look after it?

JOHNNY. I ain't got a clue.

PHAEDRA. Well, you better learn, hadn't you? If it's a gift, you gotta look after it. It's yours now. What do you suppose they eat?

JOHNNY. Search me.

PHAEDRA. Well, you've got to find out. You got to feed it. Name it and everything. Look at it. Just swimming around in there. In a bag. Just swimming back and forth. What you gonna call it? Come on. What's its name?

JOHNNY. I don't know its name.

PHAEDRA. Think of one. Come on.

JOHNNY. It shall remain nameless in honour of the boy what left it.

PHAEDRA. Everything needs a name.

She takes a pin from her costume and pricks the bag. The water starts to fountain out in a fine spray.

What's its name. If you can't think of a name before this runs out, that fish is a goner. Come on… What's its name?

She holds the bag so that the water falls upon his face. He closes his eyes.

Hurry up. Time's running out.

He takes her wrist, gently takes the goldfish from her.

You better look after that. It's yours now.

JOHNNY *goes inside. Runs the tap.*

That window in the back room's stuck. It's stuffy. There's mildew all over it. Looks like it's been there for years. Not exactly a palace, is it.

He comes back out. The fish is in a bowl. He puts it on the table. She watches it swim about.

What you stuck here for, anyway? I thought gyppos went all over. It don't make sense. Why, if you could be anywhere, why you anchor up in a shithole like Flintock?

JOHNNY. Flintock's no worse than anywhere else.

PHAEDRA. Don't say that. That's well depressing.

JOHNNY. It went like this. I travelled the four corners of the globe, from Clacton-on-Sea to Shanghai and back up to Timbuktu, then I was passing by here on a day, and I thought, 'I know this place. Feels like I've been here before.' And I parked up in this wood for the night, but getting it down that slope from the road, I hit a tree, and when I tried to leave in the morning, my axle was broke. I thought, 'I'll fix that. I'll fix that tomorrow morning and be on my way.'

PHAEDRA. You expect me to believe that?

JOHNNY. I don't expect nothing from you, fairy.

PHAEDRA. Don't you get lonely?

JOHNNY. How can I? You rats never leave me alone. When I am, I can always talk to the trees.

PHAEDRA. You ever see one? Here?

JOHNNY. One what?

PHAEDRA. A real fairy. Or an elf. In this wood? You ever see one?

JOHNNY. I've seen a lot of strange things in this wood. (*Beat.*) I seen a plague of frogs. Of bees. Of bats. I seen a rainbow hit the earth and set fire to the ground. I seen the air go still and all sound stop and a golden stag clear this clearing. Fourteen-point antlers of solid gold. I heard an oak tree cry. I've heard beech sing hymns. I seen a man they buried in the churchyard Friday sitting under a beech eating an apple on Saturday morning. When the light goes, and I stare out into the trees, there's always pairs of eyes out there in the dark, watching. Foxes. Badgers. Ghosts. I seen lots of ghosts. (*Beat.*) I seen women burn love letters. Men dig holes in the dead of night. I seen a young girl walk down here in the cold dawn, take all her clothes off, wrap her arms round a broad beech tree and give birth to a baby boy. I seen first kisses. Last kisses. I seen all the world pass by and go. Laughing. Crying. Talking to themselves. Kicking the bracken. (*Beat.*) Elves and fairies, you say. (*Beat.*) Elves and fairies.

PHAEDRA. Look at that. It's five to six.

JOHNNY. So?

PHAEDRA. I'm only the May Queen till six o'clock. After six, that's that. I'm just Phaedra Cox again.

JOHNNY. I won't think no different of you, I promise.

PHAEDRA. I can't believe that's one year ago. I was dead nervous before. Like I had a stomach full of squirrels. And the man walked along and he put his hand on my shoulder, and said my name into the microphone, and everyone started clapping. And they crowned me. I thought I was gonna faint. I rode on the winning float. Everyone cheering. Got chocolates. Flowers. I went home that night and put the crown on top of the telly. I went to bed and I thought, 'I've got a whole year now. Picture in the paper. All that ahead of me.' Not any more. Now I've only got five minutes. (*Pause.*) We should do something.

JOHNNY. What like?

PHAEDRA. I dunno. Something special.

JOHNNY. What would you like to do, Your Majesty?

PHAEDRA. I don't know. Think. Wait.

She goes over to the record player.

Do you want to dance?

JOHNNY. Not on your life.

PHAEDRA. Don't you like me? Liar. I seen you looking at me. You like me just fine.

JOHNNY. You should watch yourself. You should get yourself away, lass.

PHAEDRA. What if I don't want to? You can't make me. I'm still your Queen.

JOHNNY. Are you now?

PHAEDRA. Yes I am, gyppo. And as your Queen, I command you to dance with me.

He laughs.

JOHNNY. I don't dance.

PHAEDRA. You don't have no choice. I command you. It's a royal command. Come on, gyppo. Come on. Dance with the May Queen.

She puts on music. She starts to dance. She takes his hand, he stands up. They dance together.

They stop, looking into each other's eyes. Close. Suddenly she turns and flees.

JOHNNY *turns.* TROY *and another two* MEN *are standing there. One has a blowtorch and a branding iron.*

JOHNNY *stretches his arms wide, smiling. They run at him. Grapple him to the ground, force him inside.*

TROY *guards the door. From outside we can hear and sense an awful beating taking place.*

GINGER *enters the clearing. He can hear the fight.*

Silence. Then a single bellow of pure pain.

And again. GINGER *turns and runs.*

Eventually the door opens and the MEN *run away. The song ends. Sounds from the fair drift across the clearing. Applause. A Tannoy. The Mayor's speech. We can't make out the words. But laughter is heard. It's dreamlike on the wind.*

JOHNNY *comes out. He stumbles down the steps. He has broken ribs. Wrist. He's bloodied. Bleeding from his nose. On both cheeks, charred and bloody 'X's.*

Breathless, JOHNNY *collapses against the chicken coops. Breathing hard.*

GINGER *re-enters.*

GINGER. Rooster. You all right? (*Pause.*) Rooster? I seen Troy Whitworth running off. What they do? Mate? What they do to you?

Pause.

JOHNNY. William Blake. (*Pause.*) It was William Blake.

GINGER. What they do, Johnny?

JOHNNY. Don't come near me.

GINGER. Mate –

JOHNNY. I said stand back.

GINGER. Johnny. There's two dozen South Wiltshire on Upavon Road. They got shields and batons. They're tooling up. They got an army. They're coming here.

JOHNNY. An army, you say? Well, you better get home, Ginger. Get away from here.

GINGER. What you talking about? I'm staying here with you. If there's a fight, I'm staying.

JOHNNY *laughs.*

JOHNNY. You're staying, are you?

GINGER. Yes, mate. Never leave a man on the ground.

JOHNNY. Oh, Ginger. Ginger. Ginger, lovely Ginger. (*Beat.*) What do you want from me?

GINGER. What?

JOHNNY *struggles to his feet.*

JOHNNY. I mean, really, why the fuck are you still here? Your lot cleared off years ago. You're still here. Year in. Year out. Why? Seriously. Why are you still here. Why the fuck are you still here?

GINGER. I thought we were mates.

JOHNNY. Mates.

GINGER. I thought we were. Friends and that.

JOHNNY. I see. I see. Well. Listen to me now. Listen very
carefully. (*Beat.*) We're not friends. I'm not your friend. I'm
Johnny Byron. I'm nobody's friend. Is that clear? Now get.
You and all these rats. Just leave me alone. Or yours is
what's coming.

GINGER. But –

JOHNNY *picks up the poker from the barbecue.*

JOHNNY. I said, get away.

GINGER. But –

JOHNNY. Away, I said. I ain't fooling, boy. Get away.

Pause.

GINGER. Once a cunt, always a cunt.

GINGER *turns and leaves.* JOHNNY *drops his poker.
Sounds of applause drift over from the fair.* JOHNNY *wipes
his face. He turns around.* MARKY *is there.*

What do you want?

MARKY. I got lost.

Pause.

JOHNNY. Come here. (*Pause.*) Come here. I won't bite.

He does.

What did you do? Did you go on… go on the whirler-
swirlers? Have – Coke, Coca-Cola?

MARKY. Yes.

JOHNNY. It's all right, boy. Don't be scared. Here. Sit down.
On that.

MARKY *sits on the drum.*

There. Now, there's something I'm gonna tell you. Your
mum won't like this, so listen hard, because I'm only tellin'
it once.

He lights a cigarette. Wipes his nose, shows MARKY.

See that. That's blood. And not just any blood. That's Byron blood. Now, listen to me, now, and listen good, because this is important. (*Beat.*) I used to jump. Across Wiltshire, southwest. All over. One day here, ten thousand people showed up. In Stroyer's Field, half a mile from here, they lined up thirteen double-decker buses. Fair Day like today. But wet. Raining. The ground was soft as butter. Stroyer's Field slopes left to right and it's rutted. On the day, the wind was blowing straight down the field. (*Pause.*) And I raced down the ramp. And I took off. I hit that last bus so hard my boots came off. That's what they want to see. They want to see you shatter some bones. Swallow all your top teeth. Tongue. And when they get you out after an hour and four heart attacks, they want to see the ambulance get stuck in the mud halfway across the field. When I got to the hospital they found something out. I've got rare blood. Rarest there is. Romany blood. All Byrons have got it. I've got it and you've got it too. Listen to me, now. This blood, it's valuable. To doctors. Hospitals. Every six weeks, I go up Swindon General, and I give 'em a pint of my blood. And they give me six hundred pound. They need it, see, and I'm the only one they know's got it. (*Pause.*) And when I sit in that waiting room, waiting to go in, they treat me like a king. I can sit there, with the other patients all around, and I can smoke, have a can, right there in front of the nurses. And they can't touch me. People complain. They can't touch me. They need me. See. They need me. So don't ever worry, because anywhere you go. If you're ever short. Back to the wall. Remember the blood. The blood.

He kneels in front of his boy. Clasps his shoulders. Holds his eye.

School is a lie. Prison's a waste of time. Girls are wondrous. Grab your fill. No man was ever lain in his barrow wishing he'd loved one less woman. Don't listen to no one and nothing but what your own heart bids. Lie. Cheat. Steal. Fight to the death. Don't give up. Show me your teeth.

MARKY *does so.*

You'll be fine.

JOHNNY *hugs* MARKY *to him.*

Now go find your mother. Go on. Get.

MARKY *heads off. A Spitfire flies over.* JOHNNY *goes around the back of the caravan. He reappears with a can of petrol. He splashes it around the inside of the caravan, and on the outside too.*

> I, Rooster John Byron, hereby place a curse
> Upon the Kennet and Avon Council,
> May they wander the land for ever,
> Never sleep twice in the same bed,
> Never drink water from the same well,
> And never cross the same river twice in a year.

He picks up a handful of the ashes of the petition. He limps around the clearing, dropping piles of ash.

> He who steps in my blood, may it stick to them
> Like hot oil. May it scorch them for life,
> And may the heat dry up their souls,
> And may they be filled with the melancholy
> Wine won't shift. And all their newborn babies
> Be born mangled, with the same marks,
> The same wounds of their fathers.
> Any uniform which brushes a single leaf of this wood
> Is cursed, and he who wears it this St George's Day,
> May he not see the next.

He stops in the middle, by the drum. Closes his eyes. And begins to incant.

Alfrid Byron. Egbert Byron. Oswin Byron… Sebbi Byron. Swidhelm Byron. Wilfrid Byron. Gilbert, Bennet, Thomas Byron. Rolande, John, John, William Richard Georgius Byron. Gregorius Robert Byron. Jonas Petrus Byron. William Malet Byron. Geoffrey Aimery Byron. Francois Byron. Wardard Vital Byron. (*Suddenly calls.*) Surrender,

South Wiltshire! You are outnumbered. I have you
surrounded. For at my back is every Byron boy that e'er was
born an Englishman. And behind them bay the drunken
devil's army and we are numberless. Rise up! Rise up,
Cormoran. Woden. Jack-of-Green. Jack-in-Irons.
Thunderdell. Búri, Blunderbore, Gog and Magog,
Galligantus, Vili and Vé, Yggdrasil, Brutus of Albion. Come,
you drunken spirits. Come, you battalions. You fields of
ghosts who walk these green plains still. Come, you giants!

*Relentlessly he beats the drum. Faster. Faster. Staring out.
He pounds on and on until the final blow rings out and...*

Blackout.

Curtain.

The End.

A Nick Hern Book

Jerusalem first published in Great Britain as a paperback original in 2009 by Nick Hern Books Limited, 14 Larden Road, London W3 7ST, in association with the Royal Court Theatre, London

Reprinted with a new cover in 2010 (twice), 2011 (five times)

Jerusalem copyright © 2009 Jez Butterworth

Jez Butterworth has asserted his right to be identified as the author of this work

Cover photo: Simon Annand
Cover image design: aka
Cover design: Ned Hoste, 2H

Typeset by Nick Hern Books, London
Printed and bound by CPI Group (UK) Ltd, Croydon, CR0 4YY
A CIP catalogue record for this book is available from the British Library

ISBN   978 1 84842 050 2